Mother-in-law Hell

Mother-in-law Hell

Real Stories about Real Mothers-in-law

Patricia Bachkoff

Writers Club Press
San Jose New York Lincoln Shanghai

Mother-in-law Hell
Real Stories about Real Mothers-in-law

Writers Club Press
an imprint of iUniverse.com, Inc.

For information address:
iUniverse.com, Inc.
5220 S 16th, Ste. 200
Lincoln, NE 68512
www.iuniverse.com

To protect the privacy of the daughters-in-law who shared their stories for this book, all names have been excluded. Also, to prevent the war of the century, the identities of both my husband and myself have been altered for this book. I will refer to my husband as Chris, and you can try to figure out which mother-in-law horror stories are mine.

ISBN: 0-595-12899-8

Printed in the United States of America

This book is dedicated to all of the daughters-in-law who took the time to write their story and share it with me. You will never know how much each one of you helped me realize that I was not alone in this unspoken struggle. Once you read these stories, I am hopeful you will recognize that many other women, like yourself, are trying to cope with the same feelings of anger, frustration, guilt, and sadness.

SHARE YOUR STORY

Do you have a mother-in-law story that you would like to see published in the 2nd Edition of Mother-in-law hell? Daughter-in-law? If so, I invite you to visit my website at:

http://www.themotherinlaw.com/ to submit your entry.

While you are there, please take a look around the one and only Daughter-in-law Information Portal. I hope that you will become part of our community. You can also email your story to: **support@themotherinlaw.com**

CONTENTS

PREFACE

I have been collecting mother-in-law stories for the past year. In the beginning, I was doing it for self-therapy. My mother-in-law was mean, jealous, spiteful, and domineering. She treated me like a monster who had come into her life and stole her baby boy away from her. She made me feel like an intruder, even when I was in my own home. If I knew my husband and I were going to see her, I would get a knot in my stomach from nerves. I truly did not know what I could have done to make her hate me.

Although I was able to speak about my mother-in-law problems with my friends, no one can fully understand what it feels like to be despised by your husband's mother. Then, you have people tell you things like "You can't get between your husband and his mother" or "Just deal with it and ignore her." That is easier said then done! I think the thing that frustrated me the most was that I didn't deserve to be hated by her. All I did was fall in love with her son. I guess that was reason enough.

After being tormented by her for over three years, I was at my breaking point. I either had to completely distance myself from her, or I had to leave my husband. Of course, I didn't choose the latter, and I cut off all communication with my mother-in-law. At first, I felt empowered. I had won this battle. However, soon after I stopped speaking with her, my husband did too. I never asked him to do that, but he said that she had hurt him by hurting me. I felt so guilty for tearing my husband and his mother apart.

At this point, I felt lost, and I had no one to turn to. That is when I decided to seek the advice and support from women who may be or have already been in the same situation as myself. The response was overwhelming. After reading the hundreds of stories that were sent to me, I realized that I was not alone nor was I to blame. You will be surprised to see how many other women, like yourself, are suffering in silence while their mothers-in-law continue to negatively affect their lives. These stories helped me heal, and I hope they do the same for you.

ACKNOWLEDGEMENTS

I would like to thank my mother for the knowledge, laughter, and happiness that she has blessed my life with. Thank you for teaching me to stand up for myself and to never walk on eggshells for anyone. Not even for you. Most importantly, I want to thank you for showing me unconditional love and for never trying to stand in the way of my dreams. I should also thank you for being a great mother-in-law to my husband! I would like to thank my husband for supporting me in this endeavor. Without your encouragement, this book would have been just another project I left unfinished. And although my life could have been less stressful if I did not have to deal with your mother, it would not have been complete. We have our ups and downs, but we always seem to remember what is truly important to us. You will always be my best friend and the love of my life. Last but not any less important, I would like to thank my family and friends for listening to me through my years of mother-in-law blues.

A LETTER TO MY MOTHER-IN-LAW

Dear mother-in-law,

I don't understand why you hate me so much. I love Chris with all of my heart. In the beginning, you seemed to like me. Maybe you liked me because I wasn't a threat yet. Although you have a daughter of your own, you use to tell me that I was the daughter you never had. Then, something drastically changed.

Once you realized that Chris and I were serious about our relationship, I became your enemy. You made me feel like we were in competition with one another for his attention. The same way that two girls fight for the attention of the boy they like. In my mind, you were his mother, and I was his girlfriend. Nothing more and nothing less. Soon after, you began to do things that made me feel uncomfortable when I was around you.

For instance, whenever I was around, you would speak in Spanish to Chris. Although I don't understand the language very well, it wasn't difficult for me to figure out that you were talking about me. You speak English fluently. Also, why did you try to make me jealous? When I would come over to wait for him to come home, you would tell me that he was out with another girl. You and I both knew that he was at work. If you loved your son and knew how much he loved me, why did you try to get me to break up with him?

I know you feel like I purposely took your son away from you, but it is the furthest thing from the truth. I have such a wonderful relationship with my mother. Why wouldn't I want my husband to have the same relationship with his mother? You can blame me until you're blue in the face, but it will never take away the hurt you caused Chris.

You said that I was brainwashing him. How do you think that makes a man feel? Do you think that he is so weak-minded that I was able to cast a powerful spell on him? Also, if I had the capability to brainwash people, don't you think I would be making a fortune off of my magnificent powers? I want to spend the rest of my life with your son, and there is nothing you can do to prevent that. We plan to have children in the future, and you will not be a part of their lives. Unless you change your ways, I refuse to subject our children to your dysfunctional behavior. Don't you want your grandchildren to know who you are?

I am not asking you to like me because that would be asking way too much. In your eyes, I am a monster who possessed your son to hate you. How could you ever like someone as evil as me? To tell you the truth, I could never like you either. I think that you are a very mean-spirited, unhappy, and controlling witch, but I am willing to tolerate you for my husband's sake. That is what love is all about. I made vows to take the good with the bad. He is the good, and you are the bad.

For a long time, I believed this was entirely my fault. Then, I communicated with other daughters-in-law from around the world. We share similar problems. Many of their mothers-in-law behave just like you and even worse. You all seem to be made from the same mold.

Here are their stories…

Part 1: In the Beginning

At what moment did you realize that you had the mother-in-law from hell? When did you begin to recognize her subtle yet sarcastic remarks to you? Did it come right after her son put the ring on your finger and said "I Do"? When I was writing this book, I needed to re-live my personal experiences that I had with my mother-in-law. In doing this, I began to remember small but significant instances and comments that she had said and done to me during the course of our courtship.

For example, my husband and I had been best friends for about a year before we starting dating. One night, we were going out to see a movie, but Chris had to stop by his house so he could change out of his work clothes. At this point, I had never met his mother. He introduced me to his mother, and then he went into his bedroom to change. Thinking back to this night, I felt very nervous around her, and I am not one to be easily intimidated.

Anyway, she asked me if I was dating her son, and I told her that we were co-workers and friends. I thought that would be the end of the conversation, and she would go back to watching TV. Then she says, "I knew that my son wasn't dating you. He dates skinny girls, and you're chunky." I wanted to drop dead right there on her Living Room floor? Have you ever heard of such a thing!!

I can almost guarantee that if you went into your mother-in-law memory files, you will find some of these stories too. I believe that if your mother-in-law does not like you now, she probably never did. After you read this selection of stories, you will see that your battle began way before she officially became your mother-in-law.

LOVING YOUR SON A BIT TOO MUCH

I have the future mother-in-law from hell. She is a living nightmare. She always confided in me about all of the qualities that she looked for in a man and why her first two husbands' didn't quite make the cut. When she would get too involved with a man, she would dump him because he wasn't "perfect". I mentioned to her that I felt very fortunate to be in a relationship with her wonderful son. She responded by saying that if I weren't in the picture, her son would be the man for her. I nearly died.

Since that conversation, I feel so uncomfortable around her. She even has this sick idea in her head that she is going to stand at the altar with us and say our wedding vows. After announcing our engagement to his family, we began discussing little things about the wedding that we, as the bride and groom, wanted.

As soon as we started talking about our honeymoon destination, she decided that we should make it a family trip. We told her that we didn't think it would be such a good idea. The minute after we told her this, she declared her hatred for me. She also expressed her great disappointment in her son for choosing to spend the rest of his life with me. She won't eat meals with me anymore, but she still comes over to our house all the time. And she still demands that we take her on our honeymoon.

EVIL IN DISQUISE

I despise my future mother-in-law with a passion. She is the most evil and controlling freak I have ever had the displeasure of knowing. She hates me and doesn't condone my marriage to her son. One reason she dislikes me is because I am afraid of dogs. She said I am not normal and can't understand why her son would want to marry someone like me. She doesn't know anything about me at all! Freak! Freak! Freak!

We went to a wedding this past week, and she tells her son that she wants to take a picture with me! For what damn sentimental reason I don't know! She is always putting on this goody-two shoes act. Everyone thinks she's Miss Friendly, but I don't fall for her phoniness and refuse to play her stupid games. The next day, she told her son that I was so rude to her at the wedding, and he didn't even defend me. I hate her so much. How could I ever talk to her or be civil with her if I can't even stomach the sight of this woman? As far as I'm concerned, she should just crawl back under the rock she came from!

MUMMY DOESN'T THINK MUCH OF ME AT ALL

This woman is not even my mother-in-law yet, and I am already having a hard time dealing with her. She has destroyed the relationship between her daughter and her son-in-law, and now she is working on me. She is constantly spreading rumors about me around the small town we live in, and this is causing problems for me. Also, she has tried to setup my boyfriend with another girl right in front of my face.

Truthfully, I should have seen this coming anyway. Several years ago, he told me about his break-up with his ex-girlfriend and how his mother rang her and tried to work out the relationship for them. Mind you, the EX was a very nice Ethnic girl that "Mummy" wanted for her little boy! Bottom line is, I just can't compete, and I won't try to conform to her standards. Why do mothers-in-law have to be in everyone else's business?

CRUEL INTENTIONS

When my husband and I first got together, his mother was ecstatic. She loved me and thought that her son could do no better. She was as sweet as could be until she realized that her son was falling in love with me. From that point forward, she was so hateful. One day, my mother-in-law cornered me at the place she worked and started screaming at me. She said, "My son doesn't love you, and he never will. If you have marriage or children planned in your future, then you better run along and find another man. My son doesn't want to get married, and he definitely doesn't want to have kids with you. In fact, my son told me that the very thought of having sex with you repulsed him." I knew she was lying and that she was just trying to scare me away from her baby boy. Much to her dismay, we are happily married and expecting twins. I am never rude to people, but she is one woman I don't have a problem disrespecting.

CHAMPAGNE TEARS

The first time I met my mother-in-law was on Holiday. Her son and I were suppose to stay at her home for two weeks but ended up staying for only two days. On the first day of our visit, I asked her in a friendly and cheerful voice if she wanted me to call her Bridgett or Bri? She told me that I could call her Mrs. Johanson. That evening was New Years Eve. At the stroke of Midnight, we popped the cork of the champagne bottle and prepared to toast everyone into the New Year. Instead, my mother-in-law looked directly at me, burst into tears, and ran out of the room. We left the following morning. Since then, she has warmed to me, but what choice did she really have? My husband and I have been happily married for over ten years now.

KNOWING WHEN TO LET GO

My boyfriend and I have been together for five years. The only arguments we have always seem to involve his mother. Life with my boyfriend would be ideal if she would stop trying to ruin my life. It has been her mission to destroy our relationship ever since she found out that I was eight years older than her son. I had been together with my boyfriend for a little over three months when I met his mother. She had invited us over for dinner. I thought that was a very gracious gesture, and I was looking forward to meeting her. About twenty minutes into our meal, she asked me how old I was. I thought that was a little rude, but I didn't want to ruin things on the first meeting, so I told her that I was thirty-three years old. I would never be able to give you an accurate description of the disgusted look that this witch had on her face. Then I looked over at my boyfriend, and he had his head down and refused to look up. I thought I just landed in an episode of the Twilight Zone!

I could never of prepared myself for what came next. She stood up from the table, aggressively pointed her finger at me and shouted, "**YOU ARE A CRADDLE-ROBBING PERVERT, AND YOU SHOULD BURN IN HELL FOR RAPING MY SON!**" Then she told me to get the hell out of her house. Once we were outside, my boyfriend begged me to forgive him and her. He told me that she would learn to like me in time. Well, five years later, and she has finally won. My boyfriend was going to propose to me next week. We even picked out my ring. However, those plans have changed. I came home from work today to find that he had taken all of his belongings and moved out. About an hour ago, he called me to explain his heartless decision. He said that he had gone to his mother's house to tell her that he was going to propose to me. As soon as he told her, she fell to the floor and began gasping for air. He thought she was having a heart attack so he attempted to call 911. She caught her breath long enough to tell him that she didn't need an ambulance, but she needed him to promise her that he would not marry me.

After she finished her Oscar performance, she asked my boyfriend to move her onto the couch. She needed to rest. I don't know about you, but if I felt like I was having a heart attack, I would definitely want to go to the hospital to get checked out. What a gullible jerk he is. Anyway, he told me that this incident made him realize that his mother was the most important person in his life, and he was not going to kill her just to be with me. So, he left. While he was telling me this story, I was thinking of a million things to say back to him. But when he finally finished, I was speechless and hung up the telephone. He keeps trying to call me, but I don't want to talk to him anymore. He made a choice, and now he will have to live with it. I am suffering so much right now, but in a way, I know things happen for a reason. She could have become my mother-in-law, and I would have been married to a gutless coward.

Unfortunately, love is sometimes not enough. I hope my story can help other women who are about to commit themselves to sharing a life with a mother-in-law from hell. Believe me, this is only the beginning. Please don't think that one day she is going to wake up and love you. My best advice is to see where you stand against his mother, and ask yourself if you want to always be second string. Make the decision before it's too late. I am relieved that I have. Good Luck no matter what you choose to do.

Part 2: Prenuptials

This is the time when you and your boyfriend decide to take your relationship to the next level. He has asked you to become his wife and you begin the wedding preparations. Family and friends are happy to hear the good news. They have seen the love grow between the two of you and know that you will have a blissful future together.

However, there is one exception to these ideal months. Your future mother-in-law is suddenly giving you the cold shoulder. Or maybe she is walking around as if she has just been given the Death Sentence. No matter what she is doing, it is affecting you. In my opinion, she reminds me of a cloud, and it's not the kind you may be thinking of. Picture this, you are spending a day in the outdoors, and the sky is so clear that it looks as if someone has hand-painted it baby blue. As you are breathing in the fresh air and soaking up the rays, you suddenly feel a cool breeze cover your body and the warmth of the sun is gone. You look up and see this one cloud that has covered the sun. You figure it will move along shortly, so you patiently wait. Yet, this one little cloud won't go away. It looms over you until you give up and go inside. Does this remind you of anyone? I thought so.

Some mothers-in-law just can't let go of their children, especially to a woman like you. You are not good enough for her son. Her idea of a perfect daughter-in-law would be someone who never threatens her power. She remains as the Captain, and the daughter-in-law is just another person in her Regime. Now, if you are a strong-willed woman, and you don't abide by her rules, then she will go to great lengths and stoop to the lowest of levels to prevent you from marrying her son. And if that doesn't work, then she will try to make everyone else as miserable as she is.

TAKE A STROLL DOWN MEMORY LANE

During our Engagement Party, my future mother-in-law asked me to come to the refrigerator with her because she wanted to show me something. Since she had done so many spiteful things to me in the past, I should've prepared myself for this one. On the refrigerator were pictures of every girl my husband had ever known. There were about five pictures of him at his prom, a couple at the beach, some from his school trip to Europe, and a few pictures of him in the eighth grade with some of his *girl friends*. When I told her that I thought she was a very sick person, she said that she loved these girls and just wanted her son to remember them before he gets married. Is that screwy or what?

DEEP-ROOTED PROBLEMS

I have only had a few relationships, but I have never had to deal with someone's mother Before. This is the worst! Okay, here it goes. I met my fiancé through my best friend. He is her brother so I have known their mother for approximately six years. When I would visit my best friend, I was always respectful in her home, and we got along fine. Although I knew that she didn't care for me much because she thought I was the cause of her daughter's problems, we never had any major falling outs.

Then when her son and I got engaged, she went around telling people in our area that she was going to break us up. She even went through my high school files to try and find something wrong with me. She had access to them because she was a school employee. She also tried to tell my fiancé lies about me. You name it, she did it. If that wasn't bad enough, she used to call our house and if I answered the phone, she would hang up on me.

One day, I got fed up with her bad attitude, and I screamed at her. A person can only take so much. The last and final straw was when my fiancé and I temporarily separated, and he went to live back home with her. She made it very clear that I wasn't allowed in the house. One time, I had to pick him up at her home to take him to the doctor. Mind you, I was not even out of the car when she came out of the house screaming and cursing at me and calling me a whore. She even called my mother to tell her what a dirty little slut I was along with spreading rumors about me around town.

As of now, my fiancé has not spoken to her since that incident, and it was not by my prompting. And I have no intention of dealing with her in any way. I think her problems stem from her own divorce that she hasn't gotten over yet. But to be honest, I just think she is a very mean and bitter lady who really needs help.

IT IS EASY TO SPEND MY MOTHER'S MONEY

When I was planning for our wedding, I told my husband's mother that she was allowed to invite fifty guests. Well, her list grew to about eighty people. She insisted that all of her friends have known my husband since he was a little boy and would be devastated if they couldn't attend his wedding. I had only budgeted for a hundred guests, but I didn't want to shake things up by asking her to pay for the overage. Instead, my mother fronted me the money. On our Wedding Day, my husband looked around the Reception Hall and told me that he didn't know half of the people who were sitting at the tables. As we went around introducing ourselves to her supposed closest friends, we got to meet her accountant, her hairdresser, the man who does her lawn along with his wife, and some of her neighbors.

AND SO THE FEUD BEGINS

Recently, my future mother-in-law called my mother and insisted that I should not wear a white wedding gown because I was impure. For good reason, my mother got defensive and told her that her son was the only man who made me impure, and it was really none of her business anyway. Then my mother-in-law retorted by saying, "Now I see where your daughter gets her bitchy attitude from."

PS. They have not said a word to eachother since that telephone call, and I doubt they ever will. The way I see it, my mother is definitely getting the better end of this deal.

NAME CALLING

When my mother-in-law learned that her son was going to marry me, she sat me down for a "little talk". She informed me that I **would** be allowed to call her by her first name. However, I **was not** allowed to call her Mom, Mother, or any other such thing because I was not her child and never would be! Needless to say, I was floored. All of my friends called my parents Mom and Pops. I could not believe the slap in the face she was giving me. Fifteen years later, and our relationship is not much better.

THE INVISIBLE WOMAN

At our wedding rehearsal dinner, my mother-in-law announced that she would like to make a toast. I assumed that she was going to congratulate us. Instead, she wanted to wish her son and daughter Happy Birthday. Mind you, her son's birthday was two days before and her daughter's birthday was still three days away. It just so happened to be my birthday that night, but she forgot to mention that. Then to finish her speech, she told everyone that she still did not want her son to marry me, and we did not have her blessings. She disapproved of the wedding so much that she invited seventy of her closest friends while my mother paid the bill!

THE MEANEST OF ALL

My fiancé and I were planning our wedding, and we were paying for it by ourselves. Since I had lost both of my parents by the time I was fourteen years old, I was very excited to be getting a "mom". Ha! What a joke! As we sat at my kitchen table discussing wedding plans, his mother looks over at me and says, "Flowers? You don't need flowers to get married." I told her that I had saved $200.00 for flowers, and I really wanted to have them at our wedding. She stood up, leaned over the table towards me, and said, **"YOU MAY HAVE BEEN A RICH B**CH WHEN YOUR PARENTS WERE ALIVE, BUT THEY'RE BOTH DEAD, AND YOU DON'T HAVE S**T!"** After nine years of marriage, I have divorced my husband and never have to see that woman's ugly puss again!

SHE WAS TOO LATE

My mother-in-law and I have not gotten along with one another right from the start. When my husband told his mother that he was going to marry me, she told him that she would disown him if he did that. Did I forget to mention that I was four months pregnant at the time? I had two children who were one and three years old before she finally gave us her approval.

INDIAN GIVER

Neither my mother-in-law nor any other member of my husband's family came to my wedding shower. They claim that they didn't get the invitations. Then my mother-in-law changed her story and said that she was embarrassed to attend the Shower because she didn't have any money for a gift. That same day, she asked me to go to her apartment to pick up some chairs that she was getting rid of. And there on her kitchen counter sat an unopened juice-maker with the $99.00 price tag still on the box. She had bought a gift for me, but then decided to keep it for herself.

SINNER

I have not gotten along with my mother-in law ever since the first day I met her. That was eight years ago. The wedding...where do I start? I got pregnant right after her son and I got engaged. Instead of getting married after the child was born, we decided to move up our wedding date. However, we didn't want to tell anyone that I was pregnant yet.

Well, first my mother-in-law forced my husband to call his grandma immediately and tell her I was pregnant. Then she said that if someone asked her why we decided to move up the wedding date, she would tell him or her the truth. A few days later, everyone knew about the pregnancy. She had opened her big mouth to the entire town. We felt that we had told her in secrecy, but we were obviously wrong. Then she told my husband that we couldn't get married in a church because I was pregnant, and that was a sin. She also called up my husband at my house and told him that I wasn't allowed to wear a white wedding dress because I was impure. Her daughter has been sleeping around for years, and she wore a white dress!

Meanwhile, my mother-in-law and father-in-law watch porno movies, buy dirty magazines, use sex toys, and my husband is almost certain that they are into Swinging. And she has the nerve to say that I can't get married in a church or wear a white wedding dress! The irony of it is that my husband and I were virgins when we met and have only been intimate with one another ever since.

CAUGHT IN THE ACT

My future mother-in-law barely knows me, and she already hates me. I was staying over at my fiancé's apartment when things started to get hot and heavy. Suddenly, we heard a knock on the door, and before we could even react, she let herself in with her own key. Needless to say, I did not have much clothing on (only my panties), and she saw everything! Two seconds later, she stormed out of the apartment. Shortly after, she called up her son and started chewing him out. I knew that I was doomed

Ever since that day, she thinks that I am a slut, a whore, and a bit**. She also thinks that I am a gold digger. Also, she told my fiancé that she wanted me to sign a Prenuptial Agreement, but that is when I put my foot down. Now, she refuses to have anything to do with me or the wedding that's coming up soon.

NO STRAYS ALLOWED

At my Bridal Shower, my mother-in-law told my mother's best friend, "He never asked me if I liked her, he just brought her home." She said this loud enough for everyone to hear.

ONE HELLUVA MONSTER-IN-LAW

When I met my future husband six years ago, it was love at first sight. Within a week of meeting eachother, we were already living together. I think it was this seemingly premature commitment that caused my future mom-in-law to despise me. And from the day we moved in together, her mission in life was to scare off the woman who was threatening to take away her baby boy.

The tasteless gossip started almost immediately, and as all great monsters-in-law do, she did it behind my back. All of a sudden, I was a former prostitute. I had several children who had been taken away from me by child welfare because I had a severe crack habit. I must have some sort of Amnesia or Multiple Personality Disorder because after wracking my brains, I couldn't seem to remember turning a single trick or knowing what Crack even looks like. And as for having several children, I've heard of Immaculate Conception, but I wonder if there's such a thing as Immaculate Delivery?

Even after hearing about the rumors she was spreading, I still thought I would give it a try and call her. It was early in the relationship, and I had not met her yet, so I figured I would give her the benefit of the doubt. I introduced myself on the telephone and asked her if she would like to join me for lunch. I told her that she was free to ask me anything and express any feelings she might have about me. I thought this was a good way to clear the air. She pretended that nothing was wrong and agreed to meet me sometime. That sometime never came.

Next came the phone calls; she called me at both my work and home, berating me in that catty in-law sort of way. Even at this point, I continued to remain calm and polite. After all, this woman gave birth to the man I loved. When she realized that I wasn't easily scared off, she really got creative. First, she called my boss and told her that I was infected with the AIDS virus, and that I should not be allowed to bartend.

When that plan bombed, she really got low and called animal control. She told them my house was filled with filth, and that I had thirty cats inside my home. She knew that I loved my cats and would never neglect them. After inviting animal control to tour my house and show them the vaccination records, I got a pat on the back from the Animal Control Officer. Foiled again "Mom". I should make it clear that my fiancé didn't just sit by and watch. He threw a fit with his mother and told her he was cutting her off completely if she didn't start acting her age.

The final straw was when she came knocking on my door one afternoon. I had a hunch it was her, so instead of answering the door, I got up and walked into the hallway where she couldn't see me. Sure enough, I heard the door open. I peeked around the corner, and I saw her rifling through my paperwork on the coffee table. I jumped out and yelled, **"CAN I HELP YOU?"** I scared her so badly, it's a wonder she didn't wet her pants. Once she regained her composure, she had the nerve to say that she was looking for her son. I was so angry that I said, "I don't think your son is in any of my paperwork. You have sixty seconds to be in your car and gone, or you will be spending some quality time with some of this city's finest prostitutes and drug addicts in the county jail. Needless to say, she left.

Eventually, we got married, but I didn't have the big wedding I always dreamed of. We knew that if we made a big deal, his mother would show up and try to ruin the entire day. Although she didn't find out where we were getting married, she did find out that it was happening. First, she called my husband to tell him that he was a piece of scum and if he went through with it, she would never speak to him again. When he told her it was her loss, she hung up on him. Then she called my father demanding that he stop us. When my father told her we had his full blessing and that she needed mental help, she hung up on him too.

We have been married five years now, and it has been a great marriage. We have done a lot with our lives, and we love each other more and more everyday. We are so happy, but it seems that she still can't accept the fact that her baby grew up and started his own life. She has calmed down a little, but things still happen. Just recently, I found out that she has been telling all the family that my husband is dying from being exposed to my cats, and that I'm doing this intentionally. So, it seems the saga of the monster-in-law continues. That is, unless I can find a way to sneak in her house and spike all her food and drinks with Prozac!

Part 3: The Wedding Day

The following quote was taken from a story that a daughter-in-law had submitted for this book. "A daughter is a daughter all of your life, a son is a son until he takes a wife." Although her story was included in a different area of the book, I could not have picked a better way to begin this section. The Wedding Day should be a joyous time for the Mother-of-the-Groom. However, some mothers feel that this is the worst day of her life. Maybe she feels that her baby boy is going to start a new family and forget about his own. Or perhaps, she realizes that she will not have as much control over her son. Since I am not a Psychoanalyst and this book is not about what makes a mother-in-law tick, I will just say that some of them need to seek professional help.

Before I go any further, I must give credit when credit is due. My mother-in-law did try to help me plan the wedding, and she did a wonderful job designing my party favors. They were a big hit. See, the guilt never stops. As I am writing this, I am wondering if maybe this is my fault. She did offer to go with me to pick out my dress and the decorations. But I pushed her away, and I think that hurt her feelings. Before I completely submerse myself in the "If only I would of done something different" syndrome, I must get back on track. My mother-in-law behaved rather pleasant on my wedding day, besides a few snide remarks. See, miracles really do happen.

Anyway, the majority of mothers are ecstatic to learn that their son is finally settling down. They are so proud of the man that they helped to mold. This is the "normal" way she should react. Of course, if this book was about normal mothers-in-law, then you would not be reading it, and I would not have been the Author. The following selection of stories will give you a close look inside the mind of a mother right before or after her son gets married. All of their behaviors are unique. Some mothers-in-law are very morbid, some are malicious, and some just wish they would wake up from this living nightmare. And no matter how hard they try to disguise their feelings, it does not go unnoticed, especially by the Bride.

NEVER TRY TO UPSTAGE THE BRIDE

On my wedding day, my mother-in-law wore a white satin gown with a train. She looked positively bridal! Due to my pre-wedding jitters, I honestly didn't notice her. I thought the dress was Creme, and I never saw the Train. Unfortunately, she had changed into a black dress at the reception, so I didn't get to see her in her wedding gown! When we got our pictures back, I was in shock. I called my mom, and she said that everyone was talking about how ridiculous my mother-in-law had looked.

BLACK SHEEP

How do I pick just one story when I have so many? My husband and I just got married six months ago, but all communication has now been cut off with his family. It was either them or me. Okay, Okay, I got the most vivid one in my mind: What a wonderful spring day to get married on. The flowers and bows had been neatly placed on a Gazebo in the mist of a blooming hidden garden. It was the perfect setting. Maybe I am jumping ahead of myself. A few facts before I move on.

When we announced our engagement, the soon-to-be mother-in-law pulled me aside to inform me her son would not be supporting me (I have a better paying job than him). The agreement was that the wedding cost would be split three ways between my parents, his parents, and us. It did not work out this way. The only thing we asked them to pay for was a fifty-dollar setting fee for the photographer. We were told no because they said that my parents should pay for everything.

Now, back to day of the wedding. I am hiding in the bushes waiting to walk out when the best man comes up to me and says, "We can't start the wedding, the groom's parents are not here yet". So we waited and waited and finally they showed up. After the wedding, I was informed by his parents that my parents were nothing but rude to them. By the way, my mother had taken their food order and stood in line so they would not have to do it themselves. Then, I was told that I was never going to be a member of their family and that their son really didn't love me.

P.S. This was all on my Wedding Day. It just got worse from there. I finally told my husband that he had to tell his family to leave me alone, or he could find a new wife. I am happy to say that we are still together.

MOURNING THE LOSS OF HER SON

My mother-in-law wore a black dress and veil on our Wedding Day. This was long before wearing black to a wedding was acceptable. She refused to stand in the reception line and kept telling everyone that her life was over, and that she might as well die because I was marrying her son. I could not believe how selfish this woman was being. This was her son's day, and all she did was try to get people to pity her. As you can imagine, no one at our wedding was going to feel sorry for her just because her son married me. In the end, she made herself look like a jealous little baby.

HERE COMES THE GROOM AND HIS MOTHER

Let me start by saying that I have the most wonderful father-in-law possible. He is a warm, sweet, and intelligent man. I would love to spend more time with him, but he has one problem-his wife. My husband is an only child and his mother is totally devoted to him. She has no other hobby except trying to control all of our free time, squeeze in negative comments about me, and make my life miserable. I have many stories to share, but this is my favorite.

My mother-in-law insisted on walking my husband down the aisle. They walked about two feet in front of my father and I. Once we were at the end of the aisle, rather than sit down like they were supposed to do, they made a huge theatrical production as they presented him to me with hugs and tears. I had always fantasized about this moment when my soon-to-be husband would be waiting for me at the Altar with baited breath, and then he would be blown away by his vision in white. Cheesy, maybe, but what woman doesn't dream of that moment? Instead, he was trying to peel his mother off of him. It was disgusting, and it didn't go unnoticed by anyone.

HER WISH FINALLY CAME TRUE

My mother-in-law said that she was going to wear black to our wedding because she was mourning the marriage between her son and I. This did not surprise me the least bit. No matter what I did, it was never good enough for her or for her precious son. I finally had to accept that she was never going to like me. It really doesn't matter now anyway. I am divorcing her son, and she can have him all to herself.

BLOOD IS THICKER THAN WATER

On our Wedding Day, my mother-in-law wanted one picture of her immediate family. Which meant that I, the bride, wasn't wanted in the picture. That didn't seem too bad at the time. But it was this particular picture of our wedding that was displayed in her living room. The picture was of my mother-in-law, my father-in-law, my husband, and my brother-in-law. I was extremely hurt and annoyed. Ten years later, I have kept my mouth shut about it. I have tried to ignore her for all of these years, but it's getting harder by the day. Although I am married to her son, my mother-in-law doesn't consider me family because I'm not blood- related. Therefore, I am not really related to her, and this is exactly how she makes me feel.

PICTURES SAY A THOUSAND WORDS

I am a very frustrated female with a specific mother-in-law on my mind. On our Wedding Day, my mother-in-law showed up wearing black. She knew that the colors of the wedding were teal and peach, but that didn't stop her from wearing what she wanted to. Our wedding pictures turned out horrible, and not because of her clashing outfit. In every picture that she was in, she had a mean, angry, disgusted look on her face. She was obviously very happy for us. Yeah right! However, all good things come to those who wait. A bad marriage, awful in-laws, and a divorce lead me to meet my current husband of four years, my two-year-old son, and an exploding career. I would also like to mention that I now have a wonderful and kind-hearted mother-in-law who treats me like I am genuinely part of the family.

A DAY NOT EVEN SHE COULD RUIN

While I was getting ready for my wedding in the Bridal Suite, I turned around to see my mother-in-law standing in front of my face. She said, "You're a very lucky girl, Michelle." Then she turned around and walked out of the room. It was very sinister and weird. Our ceremony was being held in an outdoor gazebo. We had communion planned for just my new husband and myself as the last part of the ceremony. It would take place after the vows, rings, etc.

Well, the otherwise gorgeous day suddenly got very windy, and I was afraid that the Church's communion goblet and plate would be blown over. So we skipped communion and ended the ceremony. By that point, we were married anyway. We walked down the aisle in a whirlwind. It blew for about five minutes before the sun came out. Right before the receiving line, my mother-in-law caught my husband alone and said, "God didn't let you finish your wedding. What do you think he is trying to say to you?" Isn't that a terrible thing to say to your son?

Then, for an entire month after the wedding, she called every day trying to find fault with our marriage. She would always ask him if he was still happy and if he is sure that he made the right decision. He usually gets angry and hangs up on her. Thank goodness that I have a husband who stands up for me. As far as I'm concerned, God was showing us that He was there, witnessing our wedding, and letting everyone know that our event was good enough to be attended by HIM.

Part 4: Holidays & Visits

Remember when you were a child, and it was the night before the first day of school. Your stomach was in knots, your body was stiff, and your brain was spinning. You would go to sleep and when you woke up the next morning, you were as sick as a dog. Did you ever stop to wonder why you had the jitters? Most likely, you were nervous and perhaps even afraid of the unexpected. The first day of school is full of surprises. No first day of school is ever the same. Can you see where I am going with this?

If you have a rocky relationship with your mother-in-law, then having to visit her is not on your top ten list of favorite things to do. I forgot what having butterflies in my stomach was like until I became involved in this tumultuous relationship with my mother-in-law. Before going to see her, I would get a lump in my throat and a knot in the pit of my stomach. Although I can describe it in words, it does not even scrape the surface of what it feels like. Only daughters-in-law who have been through this can understand what I am taking about. Put it this way, I use to think that Public Speaking was the most tormenting experience I would ever have to face. Now, I would rather speak to a stadium full of people, naked, then be forced to visit with my mother-in-law.

Although I feel the comparison of the first day of school and a visit with your mother-in-law to be an accurate one, there is one major difference. Once you arrived at school, you would see some of your friends and relax a little bit. Unfortunately, this is usually not the case when you visit with your mother-in-law. Most times, that knot in your stomach is a mere forewarning of what is actually to come. There is no way of predicting what she will do or what will come out of her mouth. You know something is going to happen, but you can never tell which one of her games she wants to play with you this time.

HER CHRISTMAS WISH

My husband and I went to visit his mother in the hospital. She asked my husband what he wanted for Christmas. Jokingly, he said that he wanted a new house. She looked at him with a straight face and said, "Get rid of that woman, and I'll get you one." She had the nerve to say this right in front of me. Mind you, I have been nothing but nice to this woman.

SHE DESERVED A FAT LIP

It was New Years Eve and about fifty people were over my mother-in-law's house. When my husband and I walked through the front door, she turned around and loudly exclaimed, "Omigod Cathy! You have gotten so fat!" Everyone at the party turned around, and I almost died of embarrassment. I admit that I had gained about ten pounds, but it wasn't like she had not seen me since my weight gain. I had been over her house a few days before the party to help her with the decorations. Anyway, as I turned around to walk out the door and leave, she looked at her guests and said, "Do you see why I don't like her? The girl is so sensitive and now she's making my son leave on New Years Eve."

NOTHING LIKE STICKING TO TRADITION

My husband has always celebrated Christmas on Christmas Eve, and my family has always celebrated it on Christmas Day. This worked out perfect. Or so I thought. Christmas Eve rolled around, and we went to my mother-in-law's house for dinner. At the end of the evening, she announced that she would be serving a formal lunch on Christmas Day. My husband told me that this was the first time she had ever done this. Big Surprise! When my husband told her that we were going to my mother's house on Christmas Day, she glared at me and said, "Why don't you go to your mother's house and leave my son with his family where he belongs."

ONE SIZE FITS ALL

Every Christmas, my mother-in-law buys me a present. That's very thoughtful of her, right? Wrong! The box always contains things like jeans in my husband's size or a pair of work boots for him. How stupid do I feel opening these presents and pretending to like them? I always smile and act like it doesn't bother me, but it really ticks me off.

HOLIDAY PRAYER

I have spent Christmas and Thanksgiving with my mother-in-law for five years. And for those five years, she always seems to forget to set a place for me at the dinner table. Her excuse for her rude behavior is that she didn't think I was coming. The truth of the matter is that she was hoping I wasn't coming. Wishful thinking!

A GIFT FROM THE HEART

My mother-in-law gave me Miss Piggy slippers for Christmas. She said that they reminded her of me. Mind you that I am not "piggy" at all, and I have more manners than all of her children put together. She actually wanted me to wear them to movie night at her house. I don't think so! Garage sale item #1.

A MOTHER'S BLIND LOVE

My husband and I had been married for only three months when we went to visit his parents. As soon as we arrived, my mother-in-law commented to my sister-in-law that marriage must have been agreeing with me because I had put on some weight. Let me point out that I had gained maybe five pounds, but I was still wearing a size four. Meanwhile, in the time that her son and I have been together, he has put on about 50-60 pounds. Do you think she has ever said a word about it? No!

SELECTIVE AMNESIA

When my husband and I use to go to my mother-in-law's parties, this is how she would introduce us. "This is my son Andy and his wife (long pause) umm… Cynthia. This is his wife Cynthia." I have been married to her son for ten years, but she still seems to blank out on my name.

MY FEET BARELY TOUCHED THE GROUND

My husband and I were going to California for vacation. When we told my mother-in-law this, she begged us to stop by for a day or two in Texas. At first, I put up a fuss because I was very aware of the cruelty I would have to endure, but I knew that my husband wanted to see his father.

Our plane landed in Texas and as we were walking down the terminal, I saw his mother waiting there. My stomach fell to the floor. When she spotted us, she ran down the terminal and embraced my husband. After she let go of him, she looked me up and down and said, "What the hell happened to you?" I gave my husband the look of death, and we were on the next flight out of there.

Part 5: Defending Sons

What do you call a man who defends his mother even when she is wrong? Although I can think of more than a dozen names to call these types of men, there is one name that is most widely used. We call this breed of man (and I use the term man loosely) a "Mama's Boy." This is the man who will always make excuses for their mother's obnoxious behavior. No matter what she does to you, he will find some way to justify it.

I thought it would be a good idea to go directly to the source. One of my very good friends worships the ground that his mother walks on. I have known him for many years, and I watched many women strike out with him because she got the thumbs down from his mother. Although he has no idea why there is a need for me to write such a book (go figure), I let him read some of the stories and then asked him the big question, why? Why would you allow your mother to talk down to your partner? Why won't you correct her when she does something completely off the wall and way out of line? Why not say to her, "Mom, I love you, but I will not tolerate you talking to the woman I love like that." You don't have to say those exact words, but something along those lines. Stand up for us! Tell her off! I better stop before I go on another tantrum.

These were his exact words. "I don't know. She's my mother. What should I do, scream at her and tell her to screw off?" Right after he said that, I picked up my books and left. I have seen the light! I don't ever remember asking him to tell his mother to screw off. However, this is how he interpreted it. These men have probably turned their heads the other way whenever the situation involved their mother, and now you expect him to stand up to her. Not a shot!

Some "Mama's Boys" eventually get fed up with the fights and nip the problem in the butt. Sometimes it works, and the mother-in-law backs off. However, it can make matters worse because it gives the mother a reason to say, "My son never use to talk to me like that. He is a different person because of her (meaning you)." This is a no win situation. His mother gave him his life. And to some men, this gives her free reign to do as she pleases, even at your expense.

IT MUST BE MAGIC

My mother-in-law and I went to the grocery store. She nonchalantly mentioned to me that her son promised her that he would never marry someone with a child. Coincidentally, I had a child from a previous relationship. I was aggravated, but I was the better woman and let it go. Now, I hear from other people that she blames me for her and her son's disagreements. For five years, my husband has stuck up for his mother. He said that she can't help talking about me, and that she is too old to change her ways. He never once asked his mother to accept me the way I am.

It is as if he is under a spell that makes him baby her. Sometimes, I hear him talking to her on the telephone, and I could almost swear he was talking to a two-year-old child. And you better believe that this woman milks it for all she can! I cannot stand her. I have tried to be her friend and give her the benefit of the doubt, but I can only overlook so much. I just can't believe that I am stuck with a mother-in-law like her!

WISHFUL THINKING

I believe that a wife can handle a difficult mother-in-law if the husband is willing to support her. I could handle my mother-in-law if this was the case, but it isn't. When her behavior is out of control, my husband tells me that she has been this way all of her life, and she will probably never change. Just once, it would be nice to have my opinions and needs acknowledged before hers. She thinks that she's the center of the universe, and that everything, including holidays, should revolve around her. Get a clue and a life mother-in-law! I have a mother who I would like to spend time with on the holidays. She is bitchy, manipulative, and she is constantly making slams at me. It gets very old. Ironically, my husband has been unemployed several times during our marriage, but she never says anything about that.

She thinks that I am responsible for doing everything and anything that would make her son's life easier. This is according to her family traditions. It would be nice to make some decisions on my own without her constant pressure to do things her way. But back to my original point. All of this would be a lot easier to handle if my husband really cared about what I want, rather than what his mother wants. If he wanted a woman to be just like his mother, then he should of took her DNA and made a clone of her.

CHILDISH GAMES

I have been married for nine years to a great man. But I must say that when it comes to his mommy, he turns into a child again. The woman could stab me in the heart, and he would defend her to the end. Even if I was bleeding to death, he would say, "But honey, I'm sure it was an accident. She wasn't trying to kill you!" My relationship with my mother-in-law started out quite well. Then about seven months after we were married, I had our first child. This is when my relationship with her went sour.

Here is just one example of the many things that she has done to me. She told everyone that I was pregnant before I got married. She knew that our baby was born premature, but she was just trying to ruin my good reputation. Since I live in a small town, most people knew that our baby came early anyway, so my mother-in-law made an ass out of herself. You would think that my husband would have been a little angry with her since it reflected on both of us, but he didn't say a word to her. In the end, this is just one more thing that she has gotten away with.

Part 6: Granny Dearest

When I hear the word "Grandmother", good thoughts usually come to mind. To me, this is a woman who is loving and warm, and showers her grandchildren with attention. I should mention that I never had the good fortune of meeting either one of my grandmothers. Both passed away before I was born, so the above description may be incorrect.

In any case, I am thankful that this is one section of the book that I cannot relate to yet. I use the word "yet" because I could very well be in this predicament when I have children. So many different questions come to mind whenever I think about this. Will my mother-in-law want to bury the hatchet with me once and for all so we can become one big happy family? And what if this doesn't happen? Is she going to say bad things about me to my children? Or will she decide to have nothing to do with them because they are a part of me?

Even though I wouldn't want her negatively rubbing off on our children, I think I would still want them to know her. I guess I have weak spot for the whole grandmother figure, and I know that I am not the only one who feels this way. Many of the women who submitted stories for this section said that they didn't care anymore that their mothers-in-law treated them poorly as long as they loved their grandchildren.

Why would we want our children around a woman who doesn't like us? Since I do not have children yet, I feel that I cannot answer this question without sounding like a hypocrite. The one thing I do not like is when people try to give advice on something they have never experienced. Once, I went to a Psychologist to figure out how I could resolve the problems between my mother-in-law and me. She told me that I needed to remember that this was my husband's mother, and I should keep an open heart and ear to her feelings. I asked her if she ever had a mother-in-law and her answer was "No". She had never been married.

I just paid over $150.00 to get advice from a woman who never had a mother-in-law! I felt like a complete moron. At that moment, I made the decision to never give advice on situations I have not experienced or have knowledge about it. What I am willing to do is to picture my life with children and ask myself if I would want my mother-in-law around them.

The answer is "yes". Why? Maybe I do not want the guilt of telling my children that the reason they never spent time with their grandmother was because she did not like me. Perhaps, I know what it feels like to never have a grandmother, and I would not want to deprive my children of that too. We can look at this from so many different angles and points of view. This is a very complicated subject and much to involved to explore for this book, so I think I will leave this area to the "experts". For now, read the stories and know that many other women are right here with you.

WE ALL NEED A MOTHER-IN-LAW LIKE HER

Almost three years ago, I found out I was pregnant. I already had a two-year-old daughter. My mother-in-law was not too excited about me having a second child with *her* son. Anyway, I started to have some major problems with my pregnancy. Within a few days, I knew that I was miscarrying my baby. My mother had gone out of town and was at least six hours away from our town. My husband tried calling everyone to see if they could come help us out by taking care of our two-year-old, so that he could take me to the hospital.

As a last resort, my husband called his mother, who happened to be shopping at the mall with her nieces. He called her on her cellphone and asked her to come to our home and watch her grandchild for a few hours so we could go to the hospital. Her response was that she didn't think she could handle a two-year-old child at the mall. Here I am losing my second child and in extreme pain, and she can't quit shopping long enough to come and help us out in an emergency. My husband called my mother and she immediately headed home (six hours away). My mother got back as they were wheeling me into surgery. My husband was able to come and be with me in recovery. My sweet mother-in-law never called, visited, or showed any sympathy. She is the best!

LOVE TRIUMPHS

When my mother-in-law found out that I was three months pregnant, she cried and begged, "Don't take my son away from me." Instead of being happy that she was going to be a grandmother, she was upset that she wouldn't be able to find a way to get between us anymore. She figured if we didn't have any children, then she still had a chance to split us apart. I am happy to inform everyone that I'm still happily married to a husband who supports me and realizes how difficult his mother is. We also have a wonderful three-year-old daughter. I can't understand her. Her mother-in-law did the same thing to her, and she vowed to never come between us. Too bad for her. I found my soul mate and no matter who tries to ruin our marriage, we will always remain the best of friends.

FIVE HUNDRED MILES TOO CLOSE

When I was in labor with our son, my mother-in-law was shocked when I used the f-word during a very painful contraction, and she demanded an apology. Mind you, I was in labor for three days! Then, she started snapping pictures not even thirty seconds after I delivered my baby. Which she then enlarged and framed. You could only imagine what I looked like in them. Then, about two months ago, she sent my husband and I a letter detailing how **she** thought we should live our lives. This is coming from a woman who lives five hundred miles away. Presently, I am not on speaking terms with her.

NEVER HAPPY

When I got pregnant, my mother-in-law had a screaming fit about what an evil s**t I was for seducing her son! When my daughter was born, she had another screaming fit about how I robbed her son by not giving him a boy!

HIT AND RUN

When I was at work, my father-in-law accidentally ran over my 18-month-old son. My mother-in-law said that if the baby was a full-blooded Mexican and not mixed with Caucasian, the accident would have never happened. Although my son did not have any broken bones or internal injuries, he did spend five days in the hospital, and they never offered to give us one red cent towards the bill.

A MOTHER-IN-LAW'S OBSERVATION

I walked into my mother-in-law's house with my four-year-old daughter. Immediately, my mother-in-law starts examining her. After eyeing her granddaughter up and down, she grasps the skin on the side of her ribs and says, "God, she's skin and bones. All she needs now is some mucous running from her nose with a swarm of flies circling overhead to complete this picture." Here's another one. I mentioned in conversation with my mother-in-law that my daughter went for her first professional shoe fitting. I told her that I was surprised to find out that my daughter wears a size nine now because she has wore a size seven for awhile. My mother-in-law's response to this was, "That's nice. So now you're practicing Chinese foot-binding on my granddaughter." Isn't my mother-in-law a beauty?

IS THERE AN INHUMANE SOCIETY FOR HUMANS

My mother-in-law is so hateful. She doesn't like anyone or anything. I used to try and be nice to her, but it was no use. She hates my guts. Normally, I would have felt badly about this, but I don't think this woman likes her own kids. The only reason that her behavior upsets me is because of my children. My first child is fourteen years old, and he has only seen his grandmother one time. Our second child has never even met her, and she doesn't even know that we had a third child over ten years ago. I just wish that my children could have a nice grandmother. They deserve it. The truth of the matter is that she is the one who is missing out. Maybe one day, she will look around and see what she could have had. Instead, she will be a lonely old lady with no one around to love her. No one can stand her, not even her own children. This woman makes me sick. I wish I could just give her away.

SO FUNNY THAT I FORGOT TO LAUGH

After watching my young son play, she looked at me with a smirk and said, "Isn't it funny how the first child always looks more like the mother." I know what she meant by that and it wasn't nice. Trust me.

A HARD LESSON LEARNED

My mother-in-law convinced my husband that our baby wasn't his because she has blue eyes and blond hair, and my husband has brown eyes and brown hair. I tried to explain to her and my husband how recessive genes work. Since I have several relatives with blond hair and blue eyes, I carry the gene for that. After two years of her pressuring my husband about it, he told me that he wanted to take a paternity test. I told him that if he did this, I would divorce him. His mother told him that I was threatening him because I was afraid that he would find out the truth. In the end, he turned out to be the father (like I knew all along), and he got to have his old room back at his mother's house. I hope they live happily ever after.

OVERRULED

My mother-in-law tried to get custody of my daughter because my husband and I are not from the same race or culture. I am White and my husband is Black. She pleaded to the court that her granddaughter would have an identity crisis and grow up to be a drug dealer. The judge dismissed the case!

BAD JUDGEMENT

My ex mother-in-law didn't like me. After I married her son, I gave birth to her only grandchild. She showed no interest in him. Every time I would have pictures taken of the baby, I would always make sure to get extras for her. Yet, she never would display them in her home. I asked her about it once, and she said that she didn't have any picture frames for them. The next time I had his pictures taken, I framed a picture and gave it to her as a present. A few days later, we went to her home to visit. And on the table was the frame I had given to her with another child's picture in it. She said that it was her friend's grandchild.

BAD GENES

The most outrageous thing that my mother in-law ever said to me was directed towards my three-month-old son. We were vacationing with them in Florida. *They are extremely wealthy, don't have jobs, and spend money in a furious way.* Anyway, my mother-in-law went into a dramatic act about the day that she was born. She was telling us that she was THE MOST BEAUTIFUL BABY BORN IN THE HOSPITAL. That her mother looked down at her and couldn't believe just how gorgeous she was. Then her brother was born, and he was so ugly that the nurses wouldn't even hold him. He had hair all over his body and was so disgusting that her mother supposedly said, "Put this child back. He is too ugly to be mine!" After finishing her nauseating story, she looked down at my baby and said, "I have never noticed this before. Your son has a very strong resemblance to my brother when he was that age." UURRGGGG!!

SWEET OLD GRANDMA

My mother-in-law had a very bad habit of picking up my very young children while my husband and I were at work. I would come home, and the babysitter would be there without any kids. When I would ask her where the children were and when they would be back, she said that my mother-in-law had picked them up and didn't tell her when she would return them home. Finally, after missing an appointment with a photographer, I had a talk with my husband. He agreed that we needed to know where our children were at all times. Then we sat down with our babysitter and told her that we didn't mind the grandmother taking our children, but one of us had to be contacted.

This arrangement was fine until my daughter's birthday. I was at work and the babysitter called and said, "Boy are you in trouble!" Then she explained that my mother-in-law called to say that she was coming to pick up my daughter and take her out to buy her a new outfit for her birthday. She also informed the babysitter that she wouldn't be caught dead with a child as dirty as I (meaning me) allowed her to be. When the sitter informed her that she would need to contact me first, my mother-in-law went off on her. She cussed out the poor girl and told her that it was her grandchild and she can take her whenever she wants.

After hearing this, I called my hubby and informed him that his mother would be calling him. He said that he would have a talk with her. A little while later, he called me back and said, "I explained to her that it was OUR decision and not just yours. I told her that we needed to know where our children were at all times." He had to spend over ½ hour convincing her that I was not just trying to keep her away from our children. I called the babysitter and told her that when my mother-in-law calls back, tell her that she is welcome to pick up her granddaughter, but to please have her home by 6:00pm.for our birthday plans.

She never called back and never picked up our child. Two days later, we received a birthday card from her to our daughter. I opened it and read it to my daughter. It was a Strawberry Shortcake card wishing her a "Berry Good Birthday." Upon opening it up, I also found a small penciled in greeting to my daughter that said, "Dear Ashley, I wanted to pick you up for your birthday and buy you a new outfit, but your mother didn't want me to have you. She wants me to beg for you, and I don't beg for anything. She can go to HELL first. Love Granny and Grandpa.

Part 7: She Said What! /She Did What!

If you are reading this book, then I know you have had your share of "She Said What!" and "She Did What!" experiences. Here is a perfect example of one. I was eating dinner with my mother-in-law and my husband. As I reached for a second helping of macaroni salad, she said, "You are too fat to be eating a second helping." Without blinking an eyelash, she went back to the conversation that she was having with her son. I did manage to get up the nerve to tell her that I thought she was very inconsiderate and what she said was very hurtful. Would you like to know what her excuse was? She said that I took things the wrong way because of our language barrier. The woman has been in the United States for twenty-five years. Besides, Fat means Fat no matter what accent you say it in! The only excuse I would give her is that she is rude and has no class.

What gives these mothers-in-law the idea that they can behave so inappropriately towards us? In some cases, we could justify her actions by saying that she treats everyone like garbage. However, this excuse will not suffice. In many instances, the mother-in-law is like Jekyll and Hyde. Her friends and even other family members think she is Mrs. Wonderful. Then, when everyone has left, and you are alone with her, she transforms into a monster.

For the daughter-in-law, this can be tormenting. No one can understand why you don't get along with her, and they think that is must be your fault. You are the bad guy, and your mother-in-law is the helpless victim who has lost her son to a brainwashing witch. Her plan rarely ever fails or backfires because she is so good at manipulating people. Unless of course, you plan ahead of time and bring a tape recorder with you whenever you know that you will be around her. This way, when she tries to switch the story around and put the blame on you, you will have hardcore evidence.

P.S. Before you ever attempt this, check with your state to see if it is illegal to tape record a person or your mother-in-law without her knowledge. Trust me, she will sue you, and get a tremendous amount of satisfaction from doing so!!

SHE NEEDS MORE OXYGEN TO HER BRAIN

I have had the same mother-in-law for twenty-five years. Even though she has never really insulted me to my face, she loves to play head games with my husband. One day, we received a letter from her. Inside the envelope was a picture of her in a nightgown. She was sitting on the edge of her bed with an oxygen mask over her face. It looked like something Hannibal Lector wore in Silence of the Lambs. There was no hi, bye, or kiss my ass. Just the picture. She is a real trip. Fortunately, she has chosen to live in California, and we live in Ohio. She loves trying to make my husband feel guilty. Notice that I use the word "try".

THERE IS ONLY ONE WITCH IN THIS TOWN

When my father was diagnosed with Cancer, I had heard of a tea that was good for Cancer patients. Well, the old bat heard of what I was doing, and she started calling relatives and telling them that I was using witchcraft and voodoo to cure my father. Fortunately, my husband's other family members knew that tea was not something witches use, and they ignored her. That was pretty much the end of my relationship with my mother-in-law. It really showed me what kind of person she was. I knew she was cold, but I never thought she would stoop so low. I have not talked to her in two years, and it won't bother me if I never speak to her again. She is sick and demented.

HOME INVASION

When my husband and I were away on our honeymoon, my mother-in-law let herself into our apartment, changed out our double bed for twin beds, and then put them into separate bedrooms!

A GREEDY TUNE

My mother-in-law had a piano that she no longer wanted. We offered to buy it from her, but she didn't want us to have it. Instead, she sold it to a music store for $700.00. I was so angry that I went to the store she sold the piano to and bought it for $1,400.00. We paid double what we could've bought it from her for. My mother-in-law was so angry and hurt that she actually started to cry when she found out what we paid for her piano. She wasn't crying because she felt bad about what she did. She realized that she could have made an additional $700.00 dollars from us. What an evil person!

WHY BOTHER ASKING

This is a typical exchange of dialogue that I have with my mother-in-law.

Andrea: Did you try that new restaurant that opened around the corner?

MIL: It didn't just open.

Andrea: (Repeat the question again) Did you try it?

MIL: What place are you taking about?

Andrea: Alfred's Place

MIL: It's not called Alfred's Place.

Andrea: What is it called then?

MIL: It's not Alfred's Place. I know that for sure.

**By this point, I am too frustrated to pursue the answer. She likes to argue for the sake of arguing. Here's another one.

MIL: When are you going on vacation?

**I try to respond, but she interrupts my answer and repeats the same question to her son.

MIL: Who is going with you?

**She walks away in the middle of my sentence.

Andrea: Hey, your house is on fire!!

**She doesn't respond as I predicted because she wasn't listening to me like usual.

GREAT EXPECTATIONS

My mother-in-law sent my husband and me a picture of herself in a beautiful fur coat. We thought it was nice that she had decided to buy something for herself. Well to our surprise (yeah right), the picture wasn't the only thing in the envelope. She included the credit card bill with a $2,500.00 charge circled. You guessed it. She expected my husband to pay for the coat! At first, my husband said that it could be an early birthday gift (her birthday was only ten months away). He quickly changed his mind when I started to pack his bags.

SHE BRINGS OUT THE WORST IN ME

My mother-in-law never has anything nice to say about me. One day, my dear mother-in-law was looking at a picture of my cousin and me from high school. She pointed to my image in the picture and said, "What's her name? She's very pretty." When I told her that it was me, she said, "Oh". Then she put the picture down and nothing else was said about it. I hate to use bad language, but she's such an evil b***h, and I just hate her.

BAD MOVE

My husband and I were between houses, so we moved in with my in-laws temporarily. My mother-in-law wanted to keep everything separate. Separate foods, separate eating times, separate coffee, and separate anything you could possibly think of. One Sunday, she was in the kitchen preparing a large dinner. It was about 1:00p.m., and I offered to make dessert. I assumed that since we used to eat together on Sunday nights, this Sunday would not be any different. She continued to prepare a big dinner, and I prepared a nice dessert. At about 5:00p.m. I set the table and said to her, "Should we sit down to eat dinner now?" She looked at me, laughed aloud, and said, "I didn't cook dinner for you!" I was so angry and hurt that I will never forget it!

A TALK SHOW IN THE MAKING

My husband cheated on me with his co-worker and had a baby with her. The entire time, his mother thought that I was the one mistreating her son. Anyway, I forgave him, and we went to counseling. One night, we were watching a talk show and the topic was "My Husband Thinks I Am Too Fat". These men were calling their wives Blubber Wales, Fat Hogs, etc. I made the comment, "If I ever got fat and Eric called me names like that, I would kick him out the door!" My mother-in-law looked at me and said, "If you didn't kick him out after the affair, then you sure as hell won't kick him out for calling you a Fat Whale!" She is something else.

BELOW THE BELT

My mother-in-law and I went to see a movie together. I guess we figured that the less we had to talk to one another, the better off we would be. Anyway, when we were standing in line to get the tickets, she turns to me and says, "My son promised me that he would never marry someone with a child. How did you trap him into this." I could not fathom how someone could ask such a rude question. We were going to watch a movie together for goodness sake. Then she tried to justify her comment by saying her son was already struggling to stay afloat and now he has to take care of a child that is not even his own. By this point, I just had to shake my head and ignore her. I think her second comment was worse than the first. What she says and thinks really doesn't matter because my husband loves my child and me.

NOTHING NICE TO SAY

My mother-in-law called me on the phone yesterday to tell me something. She began the conversation by saying, "Please don't get mad. I mean this in the nicest way". Then she continued, "Your hair looks terrible. The style is so outdated". I have long straight red hair and work hard to keep it shiny and attractive. When I told her that my hubby and I both love my hair, she quipped, "Don't do it for him, do it for you!" What total bull! I told her that I liked my hair and would not be changing it. "Oh, she says, I hope you'll reconsider. It will take ten years off of you and make you look so much better." I am to the point where I no longer want to have anything to do with this woman. When my mother passed away, I thought that it would be nice to have my mother-in-law around. Boy, was I wrong. Any hopes of her being my friend or substitute mom have gone down the drain. It's a damn shame the woman has to be so insensitive.

SICK AND TWISTED

When my 12-year-old dog passed away, my mother-in-law said that she was happy the dog died. I asked her how she could say something so cruel, and she said, "Now you know how it feels to have something you love taken away from you." She was implying that she had lost her son when I married him. How mental is that?

ALCOHOL MADE ME DO IT

The first time I met my mother-in-law, she was at her kitchen table drinking a beer. My fiancé scooted me into a chair directly across from her and said, "Why don't you two get to know one another." Then he went into the living room to watch the sports channel. Before I had a chance to speak, she said, "So you're the little Barbie Doll who wants my golden boy. What do you have to offer my son? Or are you just a gold digger?" I kind of stammered in shock before saying, "Wait a minute. You just met me, and you don't know anything about me. Plus, how can I be a gold digger when he doesn't have any gold to dig for?" Just a little insight as to why I would make such a comment. My husband and I had just left our jobs, divorced our spouses, and moved to another state. Both of us had been wiped out of everything we owned except for the clothes on our back. That's a whole other story.

Anyway, my talking back to her made her angry. "Yeah, I know your type", she sneered in her red-eyed drunkenness. She scared me because she looked like a wrinkled old vulture. "You're not good enough for him." I burst out into tears and ran out of the room. My fiancé came over to the couch to comfort me, and he scolded his mother for being so harsh. She never offered an apology. Eventually, I got divorced after two years, but it was not over his mother. One thing is for sure, I was happy to get rid of her!

MAYBE SHE IS CRAZY

My mother-in-law called me four days after my breast reduction surgery. Everything was fine at first. She asked me how I was feeling and offered to cook dinner for me. At the end of the conversation she says, "I'm happy you got that surgery. I wish you had done it before your wedding. You looked like a cow that just gave birth. Your breasts were all big and sagging." I couldn't help but laugh at her insanity. As soon as I got off the telephone, I told my mom, my best friend, and my husband what she had said to me. Until this day, she vehemently denies ever saying that, and she told my husband that I made up the story so he would hate her. I think she does a good job of that on her own!

CHEAP SHOT

My mother-in-law and I were driving to my brother-in-law's house to see his newborn. On the way over there, we were making small talk, and I mentioned that I really liked Elizabeth. She is the wife of the son we were going to visit. To my surprise, my mother-in-law agreed with me. Then she actually had the nerve to say to me, "I like her too. I only wish that Joe, her other son and my husband, could have found someone just as nice!"

GIVE HER A PIECE OF YOUR MIND, SHE NEEDS ONE

My mother-in-law needs to seek professional help in every way. When I was pregnant with my daughter, my mother-in-law used to bring out photo albums filled with pictures of my husband and his old girlfriends. She also suggested that I name my child the same name as his ex-girlfriend! She seriously makes me ill. Also, my husband is so good-hearted that I think he overlooks some of the things his mother says or does to me. Many times, her comments go right over his head, or he will tell me to just let it go. What I really need to do is to tell her exactly what I think of her pompous attitude.

A BAD HAIR DAY

My mother-in-law told me that I should go to her hairdresser and have my hair done right for a change. I did go to her hairdresser and came out with a bouffant hairstyle piled onto of my head. I must have looked twenty years older. I will never listen to that woman again!

SHE DESTROYS EVERYTHING AROUND HER

My husband and I had just bought a new house, and we were tight on cash. Well, my husband's sister was getting married and there was no way that we were able to afford the airplane tickets. His sister was very understanding, but his mother threw a fit. She has plenty of money, so we asked her if she could charge the tickets to her credit card, and we would make the monthly payments. Of course, she said no, and then she came up with a brilliant idea! She told my husband to hock my engagement ring! In the end, we weren't able to attend the wedding, and his mother told his sister that we didn't really want to go anyway. His sister was so hurt by this because she had just flown down for our wedding. My husband tried to tell his sister that their mother was lying, but his sister took the mother's side. Now my husband has not spoken to his sister or his mother for two years.

IT IS ENOUGH TO MAKE YOU SICK

My husband is very sick, and he is often in and out of the hospital. One time, he told me not to call his mother because he didn't want her to know. Well I didn't call her, but someone else did. Later that day, she called me at my work screaming that it is my duty as his wife to call her! She hung up on me and when I tried to call her back, she had taken her telephone off the hook. The next day, she told everyone that I was screaming at her so badly that she had to hang up on me. Imagine, I work for a doctor and the telephone is out in the open with an entire waiting room of people. Do you think I would be screaming? We didn't talk to her for six months, but when my husband's condition got worse, she did call us.

NO RESPECT

My mother-in-law calls my husband's ex-girlfriend every Sunday. His mother is aware of the fact that my husband had an affair with this woman when I was nine months pregnant. She also knows that his ex-girlfriend continues to make contact with him via e-mail and telephone calls. Even when my husband tells his mother to stop calling her, his mother says that she has the right to speak with whomever she chooses to. What is so ironic is that his mother also had a mother-in-law who did the same thing to her, and she doesn't speak to her because of it. I haven't spoken to my mother-in-law for about two years because I feel totally disrespected.

YOU ARE SO THOUGHTFUL

Whenever my husband returns from a visit at the wicked witch's house, he always has a bag of clothing for me. His mother tells him to give them to me because the clothes are **WAY TOO BIG** for her.

SHE STINGS LIKE A BEE

My mother-in-law has said so many hurtful things to me over the course of the five years that I have been married to her son. The one thing that sticks out in my mind the most is when she said, "When I first saw you, I couldn't believe my eyes. You were not the type of girl Eric usually brought home. They were much skinnier than you." OUCH!

AT LEAST SHE'S HONEST

My mother-in-law missed my birthday. When it came up in conversation about two weeks later, she apologized and graciously explained, "I didn't really think of you as part of the family". My husband and I had been married for about three years when this happened, and I have not spoken to her since.

DIRTY MONEY

My mother-in-law told my husband that the only way she would pay for his college tuition was if he divorced me and moved back home with her. Despite her efforts, we applied for school loans, and my husband graduated college with top honors. I should mention that my mother-in-law is filthy rich.

YOU SHOULD TALK

We were at the beach and some kids kept throwing a soda can into the ocean. I got it out a couple of times for them, and then I asked them not to throw it in anymore. As I sat back down in my beach chair, my mother-in-law looked at me and said, "I don't know why you're complaining. You need the exercise so you can lose some of that weight." FYI, my mother-in-law has a butt that you can hang a billboard on!

THIS IS ONE BATTLE I AM GOING TO LOSE

My husband had an affair and now has a baby. When he confessed to me about the affair, I made him take me over to his mom's house so he could tell her. I had to be there to see her reaction. All along, she thought I was the problem spouse. We all sat down on the couch, and he told his mother everything about the affair. I thought I was going to hear her reprimand him or show some sort of disgust. Instead, the first words out of her mouth were, "Well, what do you expect a man to do when he can't get any at home!" Can you believe that? She was trying to protect him and blame his affair on me.

Part 8: The Obsessed & Possessed

In my opinion, these are the worst kind of mothers-in-law. Although these categories can be separated into two sections, I think they go hand in hand. The first one we will discuss is the obsessed mother-in-law. She spends her life fixated on her son. She wants to know what he is doing, who he is doing it with, and if he is enjoying his life without her. She always feels as if she is missing out on something, and she blames you know who!

She wants 100% of his attention, 100% of his time. Ever since her son got involved with you, she feels like she is out of the picture. Well, an obsessed mother-in-law is not going to stand around and watch you whisk away her little boy. This means war! **You are no longer his wife, but now you are the other woman.** I remember when my mother-in-law told me that her son would never love me as much as he loves her. I thought that was so sick. Of course he is going to love me as much as he loves his mother. And when we have children, he will love them as much as he loves me.

However, he will love all of us in different ways. Why would she even say such a thing? Whenever I tell my friends that story, I always compare it to the story of Oedipus and the term that stemmed from it called the Oedipus Complex. For those of you who have not heard of this before, I will give you a very simplified explanation. Basically, it suggests that a young boy lusts for his mother and hates his father. Trust me, the story that goes behind it is much more involved, and my definition is just the tip of the iceberg. However, this will suffice for the context in which I am using it. A mother can become so obsessed with her son that it appears as if she is in love with him. When you became an important part in his life, she behaved like a scorned lover. If your husband shows you affection when she is around, you can practically see the venom seeping from her veins. These mothers can be childish, irrational, and downright crazy.

Although I consider a scorned mother-in-law the worst to deal with, there is one other kind that follows at a very close second. This is the mother-in-law who wants to be the third person in your marriage. If her son has a runny nose, it is up to you to call her. Mommy does know what's best for her child. She is clingy and needy. These mothers-in-law need to get a life of their own! I feel slightly sorry for them because their entire world revolves around their sons. Her day begins at the moment she hears his voice. Ok, maybe I am exaggerating, but I want to give you a real clear image of her.

SMALL FAVORS

My husband and I got married in September. Only one day after my wedding, my mother-in-law sent me an email wanting to know when she could expect some grandchildren. I emailed her back and told her that we were not going to have children for quite some time. The following day, I received the same type of email from my older sister-in-law. The email stated that her mother would like us to have children while she is still young enough to enjoy them. Since my sister-in-law lives the closest to my mother-in-law, I told her that it might be a good project for her and her husband to work on. Then I suggested that it might be a good idea for her younger sister to have a baby. She is still in college and in much better physical shape than I am. She could probably bounce back the best after childbirth. No more was said to me on the subject.

A few days later, my husband gets an email from his mother saying, "All I want is a couple of grandchildren. I mean, it's not like I am asking your wife to cut her arm off or something. Why don't you two have one, and then just send the baby to me. I just want one for now and then you can give me the other one later." I almost passed out when I read it. The following day, I made an appointment to have Norplant inserted into my arm. I wanted to protect myself just in case my husband tried to switch my birth control pills with tic-tacs.

THE LITTLE GREEN MONSTER

One day, my mother-in-law stopped by for an unexpected visit. We had just returned from a weekend vacation, and the pictures from the trip were laying. As she was looking at the pictures, her eyes started to swell up with tears. I asked her what was wrong, and she said, "My son can take you on a vacation, but he can't take his own mother." This was not the first time that something like this has happened. My husband and I had gone out to dinner to celebrate our one-year Anniversary. His mother had asked us if we could stop by after dinner because she wanted to give my husband some clothes she had bought him. Anyway, when we met up with her, she had such a puss on her face.

My husband asked her what was wrong, and she said, " Why are you two so dressed up? Did you take her to a fancy restaurant?" When my husband told her that we went to Benihana's, she got so upset that she told my husband she was going to give his new clothes to the neighbor's son. Then she said, "Please don't tell me you love her more than me." I thought the whole thing was really weird. It seems as though she is in love with her son. She gets angry when he takes me to dinner. She practically turns green if he kisses me in front of her. Maybe I could understand her resentment if she wasn't married, but she does have a husband of her own.

TALK ABOUT SMOTHER LOVE

Shortly after my husband and I were married, my husband came down with a bad cold. As we all know, the only cure for the common cold is rest, so I wasn't panicking. Well, it just so happened that my mother-in-law called just after my husband had taken some over-the-counter medication and went to bed. When she asked where he was, I told her that he wasn't feeling well and had taken some cold medicine to help him fall asleep. She asked me how high his temperature was and then said, "He has a history of running really high temperatures, you know?" When I told her that I didn't know what his temperature was, she freaked out and told me that I had better go take it immediately! I told her that it was going to be difficult since we didn't have a thermometer.

She totally lost it and started yelling that her son was sick, and I didn't even have the decency to go buy a thermometer. Then she slammed the telephone down on me. Here is the kicker; this woman drove thirty miles from her home to ours to bring a thermometer and take her sick 22-year-old baby's temperature! Until this day, I'm amazed that she didn't stick the thermometer in his rectum. I was delighted when my husband's work moved us over 1200 miles away from her.

HER TWO FAVORITE DAYS

I have been married for five years, but I don't think that we will be celebrating a sixth year. You see, for these five years, my mother-in-law has been meddling in my life and my marriage. I guess she thinks that she has a right to do this because it involves her son. My husband and I never have any time alone with each other because she is constantly tagging along with us. The funny thing is that she doesn't even live with us. Let's do the calculations. My husband has worked for the same company for about ten years. He always has Mondays and Thursdays off of work. My mother-in-law makes sure to always have a crisis on these particular days. She will call the house early in the morning and tell my husband that she needs help doing something at her house. Her husband did pass away several years ago, so I can understand her needing my husband's help every now and then. But this happens every Monday and Thursday.

Anyway, my husband will go over to help her because he feels bad that she is alone. Well, she convinces him to stay for breakfast and then run a few errands with her. By the time he gets home, it is almost dinnertime and guess who is with him. She invites herself over for dinner. This has gone on for five solid years. She is suffocating me and I just can't take it anymore. It also bothers me that my husband doesn't do anything about it. When we finally go to lie down in bed, I ask him what the emergency was at his mother's house. Nine out of ten times, she just felt lonely. Why does he keep letting her manipulate him like this? I really wish that she would disappear and let me have my husband back.

SHE WON'T STOP UNTIL SHE WINS

My ex-husband and I got married really young, and I don't think my mother-in-law was ready to give up her son. She has done everything to sabotage our relationship. Right after we were married, I got pregnant. When I was still recovering from going through labor, my mother-in-law barged through the front door of my home. She had brought a cleaning service with her. She said, "You can live in this filth if you want to, but my grandson will not." Then she proceeded to his room and sanitized everything that wasn't bolted down! My mother-in-law was always complaining about my cleaning habits. When I would tell her that her son doesn't lift a finger to help out, she said that he shouldn't have to. She said that it's my job to keep the home clean.

Since then, her son and I have divorced, but she is still as horrible as ever. She has gone to court to try to get custody of my son, and the courts laughed her out. She has called Child Protective Services on me claiming that I am an unfit parent. She has a calendar and marks down every time my son comes over to her home with a bruise or scrape. Anytime he has a sniffle, she is running him to the hospital stating that he has been sick for several weeks, and I refuse to take him to a doctor. She buys him tons of clothes and toys but refuses to let him bring them home because I don't know how to take care of anything. She turns every situation around to make me look like the worst parent ever! Although my husband and I are divorced, there is no getting rid of her because of my son. I will be stuck with her for the rest of my life, and that is a scary thought!

BE AFRAID, BE VERY AFRAID

My husband went fishing with his father and asked me to keep his mother company. About an hour into the visit, she started in on me. She begins by telling me that my husband has always liked women with long legs, and she was surprised that he married someone so short. I am 5'4. Then she tells me that my husband used to date very natural-looking girls, unlike myself. I knew that she was trying to get the best of me, so I remained calm and didn't say a word. She became so enraged when she couldn't get a rise out of me. She started screaming at the top of her lungs that I was tearing her family apart, brainwashing her son to hate her, and that one day she is going to kill me.

Part 9: Stop Suffering in Silence

For some bizarre reason, our mothers-in-law think that they can say and do whatever they want to us, and we are suppose to take it. The sad thing is that we usually do. We do not want to start any trouble so we just back off and keep our mouth shut. But what happens when you cannot take her abuse anymore? Well, you have a couple of choices. First, you can pack your bags, run away, and change your identity to make sure that she never finds you again. Or you can stand up for yourself and not let her walk all over you anymore. Since the first choice is not very realistic or fair to your husband, I would opt for the other option. Although you may be nervous and even frightened of what the outcome will be, you need to do this for yourself.

I am not suggesting that you have a screaming match with her (it may lead to one without trying), nor do I think that you should get into a physical brawl with her. That would not resolve anything. What you need to do is "stop suffering in silence" and "find your voice". This can be accomplished in many different ways. First, if your relationship with dear old mother-in-law is at the stage when you can still come into her home (not my current situation), then I suggest that you ask her to meet with you and lay it all out on the table. There is one important thing to keep in mind: She does not like you very much right now, so you really don't have much to lose. Try not to hold anything back. If nothing else, you can excavate your body of all the negative feelings you had bottled up all this time!

Another way that you can "stop suffering in silence" is to write her a letter. Tell her everything you ever wanted to say. The letter that you read in the beginning of the book was real. I had written it after I returned

103

from a visit to her house. She had been so vicious towards me that I ended up running out of her house in tears. As I was driving home, I was thinking of all the things that I would like to do to her such as ripping her eyes out. Anyway, I decided to write her a letter and tell her exactly what I thought of her. After I finished writing it, I felt so much better. And to tell you the truth, I did not even send it to her. It wasn't necessary.

Lastly, you can just stay away from her, and not subject yourself to her abuse. No one can force you to be around her. Even if you have children, and they want to be their grandmother, you can drop them off and leave. I know this option sounds great to many of you, but then questions such as, "How do I stay away from her on the holidays?" pop into your head. Honestly, if this is the last resort, it is not going to be easy. However, if your relationship with her is this severe, then she is like poison to both your physical and mental health. You need to stay away from her for your benefit. Then it is up to your husband to decide whom he wants to be with.

The critics of this book might say, "This isn't a choice. How can a man choose between his mother and his wife?' The answer is simple. He should have nipped his mother's behavior in the beginning of the relationship. Maybe if he would have been brave enough to stand up to his mother, he would not be in this bind, and the daughter-in-law would not have needed to unnecessary suffer. So now, he must deal with it. Even if these solutions do not seem to be the right one for you, PLEASE do not continue to let her control you. As you read the following stories, you will see what happens when you do not make the choice to speak up, and then you will hear from women who said enough was enough and put an end to their mother-in-law's reign of terror. You never know, maybe after you finish this book, you will feel the little voice inside of you slowly creeping out

AN OBSESSED MOTHER-IN-LAW

Sadly enough, my mother-in-law has consumed my eighteen years of marriage. It started at my rehearsal dinner with a toast from her. "A daughter is a daughter all of your life, a son is a son till he takes a wife." This followed by crying. My mother-in-law has already gone through six husbands so I know there's a reason I can't seem to get along with her. Through the years, my husband has told me to just ignore her. It's very hard to ignore someone you see several times a week and who calls constantly.

After ten years of her stopping in every night at dinner unannounced, I had to politely ask her to call before coming over. I have had to repeat this request several times. Thank God for Caller ID. Please don't tell the Phone Company, but $5.00 a month is cheap for the relief it gives me. Also, my mother-in-law follows us everywhere. Our kids are involved in sports, and she gets the schedules from the coaches or the league and comes to all the games. If she were a normal grandparent, who acted like an adult, I would love to have her there. Also, she is so needy and obsessed with my husband that I get sick just watching her follow him around like a little puppy. She isn't a good influence on my children, so I make sure her time alone with them is limited.

My husband continues to tell me to just ignore her comments. It has been eighteen years of this hell, and I don't think I can take it for much longer. I don't want to break up my family, but how else am I going to get away from her? I went for some counseling to help me deal with my mother-in-law. My counselor sat there with a shocked look on her face and told me, "In all the years of counseling, I have never heard of a mother-in-law that was so interfering." Short of divorcing my husband, which I don't want to do, I need a way to escape from her. I feel consumed by her constant presence in our life.

GERMAN MOTHER-IN-LAW FROM HELL

My mother-in-law is of pure German heritage. I have nothing against Germans...afterall, I married her son, and I am still married to him after almost twenty-eight years. My mother-in-law goes to church every Sunday and tells everyone how religious she is. While during the week, she cuts down her own family to the roots. Anyway, ever since I met this shrieking banshee, she has made rude, nasty, and hurtful comments to me, my daughter, my son, and to my husband. I have had to go to counseling about this female Hitler. My therapist told me to avoid her because she is poison. I completely agree with her. We have a family baby shower to attend tomorrow, and she is going to be there. My stomach has been tied in knots all week.

I sent her and my father-in-law a letter three nights ago asking them to not say hurtful things to me or my daughter when we are alone with them or at family gatherings. Of course, my letter has generated no response. They have ice for blood. I have never known people who are so cold and unloving. I don't know what to do. I can't stand either one of them. The quandary is that we own a family business with them, so they are always in my face. I feel completely controlled by them and I hate them for it. This is very stressful for me to live with.

HIGH CLASS MOTHER-IN-LAW

My mother-in-law is truly from hell. Right after we got married, she told my husband that he could move back home if or when we got divorced. Shortly after giving birth to our first baby, my husband talked me into having his mother come see our newborn. He said that she was a real countrywoman and could pass on some of her wisdom to us. She showed up with her alcoholic boyfriend, and they were expecting us to entertain them. The next day, my husband had to go to work so I was left with a baby and the two of them chain-smoking and drinking beer at 9:00am. I could go on and on because I have put up with this crap for twenty years. This past year was the worst and now I want out of this marriage. Then he can go home to mommy, and I can be rid of this woman once and for all. The only reason I haven't left before is because I am afraid to hurt our three teenage children.

YOU DESERVE BETTER THAN THIS

I have had mother-in-law troubles for the past eight years. And that's pretty sad because I am only twenty-four years old. My husband and I were high school sweethearts and then we got married right after graduation. We have been married for four years and are about to have our second child. His mother says the worst things to me like, "Why are you poking out already? You don't need to poke out so much." Well, I was three months pregnant, and women do tend to show a little bit. Then five months into my pregnancy she comments, "My son likes the finer things in life. I don't know what he is doing with you."

I don't mind when she talks bad about me anymore, but when her and her husband talk about my children, this is where I draw the line. For instance, one time she said, "I didn't care much for your first child, and I am not going to care much for this one either." This is the end of trying to be nice to this woman and work things out. I am tired of her making me feel this way, and that saying, "till your mother do us part" is so true. My husband keeps defending her and tells me to just give in. He says I need to be sympathetic to her needs. Well, I don't think so, and I have had enough.

NO WAY OUT

I've been married fourteen years, and my relationship with my mother-in-law is still terrible. She is Greek and can't accept the fact that I am American. She claims that this isn't the case, but she constantly criticizes the United States and American people. When I try to defend my country, she says that I'm being too sensitive. I tend to think that anyone would become angry at statements like, "Americans are unsophisticated and uncultured." In addition, she has commented on my looks by saying, "I don't think you're that pretty."

My husband is totally worthless when it comes to putting his mother in her place. She has poisoned him with her constant guilt trips. For example, if he raises his voice to his mother, his father will say, "You made your mother cry. How could you do something like that?" Our marital problems arise from my husband's inability to defend me from his mother's arrogance and selfishness. I used to fantasize about divorcing my husband just so I wouldn't have to deal with his mother anymore. However, I have two children with him, so I must succumb to the fact that I will never get her out of my life.

She is selfish, self-righteous, cruel, and I often find myself in tears when I listen to friends speak of their great in-laws. I deserve to be liked by my mother-in-law. I have turned her son into a much kinder person than she ever did. The problem I have now is that I am desperately trying to forgive her. Yet every time I re-adjust my attitude and go in with an open heart, she slams me down again. After so many years of pain, can't I just reject her?

A WOLF IN SHEEP'S CLOTHING

I have been married for four years. I am in college and have a part-time job working with the retarded. I am also pleasant-looking and have good manners. A real catch for anyone's son, Right? NOT! When I first met my mother-in-law, she told me that she already had a "special" daughter-in-law and didn't need any more. I took it on the chin and have been taking verbal barbs from her since. I have tried humor, ignoring her comments, and have even tried standing up for myself, but nothing works. The problem is that she only says crappy things when we are alone. Most of my husband's family thinks that I am out of my mind, and she is this kind, sweet woman. She is so manipulative and so good at it that I don't stand a chance at winning her game, so I just don't play. Believe it or not, I have always been kind to her. What a **BIG** mistake that was. She views me as this weak, whipped girl because of it.

To make matters worse, I live on a family ranch in the Dakota's, so she is only five hundred feet away from me. We have no other neighbors in between us. Even though I try not to put myself in situations where I would be alone with her, you can't always avoid it when you live on the same grounds with someone. My husband supports me and believes me, but when he tries to talk to her about it, she denies everything. Basically, it is her word against mine. I feel so helpless and alone.

CONTROL FREAK

I used to get along fine with my mother-in-law, despite the fact that she and I are different in every way possible. I am a religious woman who enjoys raising a family, and my mother-in-law is an atheist, feminist and a lesbian. I have no problem with her views, but I think she has a problem with mine. First, she doesn't want my daughter attending Catholic school. She began visiting my daughter's school and getting information about her teachers and even the principle. She started offering us money to help pay for bills and whatever else we needed. At the time, her help was welcomed. Then we realized that her generosity always came with stipulations. She wanted to have say in our children's upbringing, education, and she tried to control the way we ran our household. When I decided this was all too much and removed some of her involvement in our lives and our children's lives, she decided I was mentally ill. She found out that I had taken anti-depressants for a number of years and began using that against me.

One time, she sent my husband a letter that said I was a crisis junky who likes to create problems just so I could look good by solving them. Also, she sends my husband newspaper and magazine clippings that discuss topics such as "How to Live with a Mentally Ill Spouse." She refuses to talk to me in person about it and won't read the letter I sent to her. So why is this such a problem? My mother-in-law is a well-known and respected childcare professional. She gives speeches to our community, teaches classes, and she even writes a column for the local paper.

I feel that as my mother-in-law "spreads the word" about me, people will soon look at me like I am some mental case. She is taking away my rights and destroying my life. My husband feels stuck in the middle, and his mom knows how to manipulate him. If she hangs up the telephone on him, he will spend days trying to win her over again.

THIS DAUGHTER-IN-LAW HAS BEEN THROUGH IT ALL

My sister-in-law and I were pretty close when we lived in the same town, but dear mother-in-law played conquer and divide and tried to destroy that. However, despite our Mil problems, we learned to love one another like sisters. And yes, this irritates, angers, annoys, and kills my mom-in-law. Even though she has no clue what we talk about, it upsets her that we are friends now. No one in the family, not even siblings, are allowed to like each other. She is the only Queen and there is no room for others to have relationships! When they do, watch out. She will get dive right in and make up stories.

Just a small sampling:

#1. It's 110 degrees out, and I am standing in her backyard drinking a diet soda. She hisses, "You are too fat to even think about drinking soda."

#2. I actually have a picture in my wedding album of her digging her fingernails into my arm while we were standing in the receiving line.

#3. Shortly before my husband and I married, she told him that I was a streetwalker and a slut. This is after two years of dating her son. She claimed that one of my friends told her that, and now he could not marry me. Because of her crazy delusions, my then fiancé was forced to tell her that we were both virgins when we met and have not slept with anyone else. I was mortified. It wasn't shameful news that we were sexually active, but I felt that it was no one's business.

#4. During the dating period, I went for a visit to her home. After an hour or so, my then boyfriend and I decided to go for a daytime drive in the park. No sexual rendezvous or anything. She jumped on the car windshield, clung to the wipers, and screamed hysterically for several moments. She was saying something like, "It's no fair that you get to go out and do fun things. I was never allowed to have any fun when I was younger." She did not even come from a terribly abusive family.

#5. When I was first married, she would rummage through my dirty laundry hamper for no apparent reason. The first time I found out about this was when my husband was at work. She dug out a workshirt that was destined for the washing machine and then threw it into my kitchen sink, grabbed a brush, and started scrubbing the shirt. She proceeded to tell me that my husband was going to cheat on me someday because I was a crummy laundress! Being twenty-two years old, shy, and very impressionable, I believed her! Thankfully, my hubby is not the cheating kind.

#6. And the topper! This is the one that enraged and embarrassed me the most. And even though this happened nearly twenty years ago, I found out about it only recently. I knew she was a laundry digger. Refer to #5. But what I found out from my sister-in-law is that my MIL had come across some of my underwear. These were also destined for the washing machine. My mother-in-law ran and told my sister-in-law that she had found blood in my underwear and how it was totally disgusting!

And these are mild stories! She constantly makes up outrageous lies about me, my sister-in-law, and even about her own children to a smaller extent. She takes a grain of truth and then embellishes it with her brand of lies that usually involve infidelity, lesbian affairs, and drug abuse. And the fact that she does throw in a little bit of the truth has alot of the family members suspicious of one another. She gets sympathy from her friends by telling them how rotten her children are. Of course, her kids are rotten because they married two evil women. When we went to a wedding back home, she told my husband that he was killing his father with his rudeness. And if he drops dead, it will be his fault. The dad has high blood pressure. She was just trying to get back at us because we chose to stay at his brother's house instead of with her. She is so hostile.

MAMA MIA

I have been with my husband for nine years, married for three. We have two beautiful children, if I do say so myself. However, when I look back on the beginning of our relationship, I should have run away from my husband once I found out that: a) he was Italian, b) he was HER son, and c) he was the only child of this divorced woman. What was I thinking? She offered him $20,000 to leave me, and then she offered to buy him his own store. Her bribes didn't work. Unfortunately, my husband has an extremely difficult time standing up to her. This means that I have to tolerate her speaking Italian to my husband when I'm standing right there. Of course, I know she's talking about me. She also told everyone that my husband left his Mama and moved in with me because I was pregnant. I must have had the longest pregnancy in history since our child was born five years after we moved in together!

It all came to a head when my husband and I had to move in with her while we waited for our house to be ready. My mother-in-law and I had the worst fight ever. I finally stood up to her and told her that I refuse to seek her approval any longer. She was furious and said that she wanted us out of her house. I looked her straight in the eyes and said, "I have that much power in your life that you are willing to give up your son and grandchildren?" She was speechless! That was about the last time I really gave her any of my time! I even stayed home on Thanksgiving because I refuse to be surrounded by that evil/fake thing!

IT WORKED EVERY TIME

This is how I use to get rid of my mother-in-law. I would let her watch whatever she wanted to on television. As soon as she would leave the room to eat more of my food, I would change the channel. I would turn on Univision, which is a Spanish Network. Although I don't speak or understand a word of Spanish, I would laugh at the jokes and tap my foot along to the music. She would turn beet red and yell "I'M GOING NOW." Then she would get up from the couch and storm out of the room!

UNACCEPTABLE BEHAVIOR

My mother-in-law is a manipulative witch who has dominated the lives of all five of her children. The last time she came to visit, she yelled at my three-year-old son for not giving her a hug. I had to remind her that my son hasn't seen her for over a year, and he must not recognize her. Later in the evening, it was time to open the Christmas presents. Being young children, they ripped open the packages that my mother-in-law had brought for them. She yelled at them for doing so, saying that she had intended to use the wrapping paper the following year. After criticizing everyone in the household, I lost my patience and told her to stop behaving that way or she would need to leave. She stood up, grabbed her chest, and proceeded to fake a heart attack. She even slipped on the floor in apparent agony. Sad but true. We have chosen not to let her into our lives anymore, and it's no loss. After emotionally abusing her own kids, we were not about to let her continue to force her hateful ways on our children.

SETTING THE BOUNDRIES

My first mother-in-law was running late for our wedding, so my soon-to-be husband waited for her while the rest of us went to the town where the wedding was to be held. Turns out that she had planned the whole thing. She spent the entire ride over there, *alone with him of course*, trying to talk him out of marrying me! Her plan bombed, and we were married despite her efforts. After the wedding, the problems got worse. *Strange, inappropriate hand-me-down gifts are the least of it.* Finally, I told my husband, "She is your mother, and I am not obligated to deal with her. When she calls, I will politely put you on the telephone. You can visit her, but you will be going alone. When she comes to our house, I will disappear for as long as she is here, and you can just wonder where I am spending the night!" Eventually, we divorced over other things, but we managed to stay friends. When I married my second husband twelve years later, my first husband was one of the ushers. His mother was very upset that I didn't invite her to the wedding! HA!

MY HOME, MY EGGS, MY RULES

I was making fried eggs for my husband. When my mother-in-law saw me break the yoke she said, "You fix another egg. He doesn't like when the yoke is broke, and you need to make sure you fix it just like he likes them." I told her that he would eat the eggs the way I make them now and like it! She was furious.

P.S. My husband did eat the eggs the way I made them and liked it!

I CAN LAUGH AT HER NOW

My mother-in-law lived in another state for the first six years of my marriage. Everything was fine, and she really acted as though she liked me. Then she moved to our town, and that is when all hell broke loose. In her eyes, I didn't do anything right. I was a terrible wife, mother, and stepmother. She would invite my husband's ex-wife over to her house, and they would talk about my parenting abilities. She accused me of not treating my stepdaughter right. She also went to my husband's other family members and asked them if they had noticed how I mistreat my stepdaughter. Luckily, they thought enough of me to come and tell me what she was doing. When I called my mother-in-law and confronted her about her behavior, she said, "If you think you're important enough for me to sit around talking about you, you need to think again." She never admitted to doing anything wrong.

When I finally had enough of her abuse, I stopped going over to her house. One night when my husband was over her house alone, she said to him, "If that bitch thinks I am going to kiss her ass, then she has another thing coming." Now she mostly visits or calls our home when she thinks I am at work. I have even seen her drive up to our house very slowly and when she doesn't see her son's truck, she will drive away. She could at least stop by to see her grandchildren. I used to get very upset and hurt by her behavior. Now I find it entertaining.

WORDS OF WISDOM

To make a long story short, I've had the devil herself as my mother-in-law. I have been with my husband for eighteen years, and the situation with his mother hasn't got any better from the first day I met her. She is the most evil, vindictive, venomous, plays favorites, turns everyone against each other, manipulative, and malicious person I have ever met. She has to be in total control twenty-four hours a day, seven days a week. She controls her kids like puppets and they are well into there thirties and forties. I have been nothing but nice to my mother-in-law for my husband's and kids' sake. However, that all changed when my thirteen-year-old child came up to me and said, "Don't worry Mom, Nana is half dead." I was stunned. I thought it was awful that my children knew how much she hated me. I concluded that if your mother-in-law hates you, she always will, so forget it, and go on with your life. To anyone that doesn't have a mother-in-law, consider yourself lucky and just take it from the rest of us. I am sure there are some good ones out there, but they are few and far between.

I FOUND MY VOICE

Anyone who really knows me is aware that my mother-in-law has given me enough stress to kill somebody. And I have only been in this family for nine years. It is no wonder that her children are emotional morons. In nine years of trying to love her and find her good qualities, I am coming up empty. After I delivered my third and final child (three kids in four years...you would quit too), I was emotionally and physically drained. All I could manage to do was change diapers on two children, breast-feed one, stop fights, and feed everyone. The cleaning happened when I got a spare second. Every mom and dad reading this completely understands what I'm talking about. And those of you who don't get it, either live in a fantasy world or have a maid.

My mother-in-law and father-in-law got together with my best friends to discuss my cluttered house, my marriage, my depression, and how awful I was at everything. No exaggeration here either. One of my friends was horrified and came over to my house to tell me every detail of what went on. I was the laughing stock of the family. I told my husband what happened, and he had no opinion or backbone about the matter. I told my husband, "If your mother doesn't like it here, she doesn't have to come over! And if she is so concerned about the cleanliness of our home, then she should've gotten her fat ass over here and cleaned the damn house for me!" I was so hurt and angry that my husband didn't take my side.

Although I was angry, I don't hold it against him...anymore. How can I? Look at what he has for a mother. Anyway, I confronted his family and brought up everything that has ever bothered me. This went down while my husband listened and never said a word! I started out calm, but then it got worse. I ended up being known as the screaming woman on the corner. I have no problem with it. My mother-in-law admitted to me that she loved her grandchild from her daughter better than all of my kids. The gall it takes to say something like that still astounds me to this day. I know how people can show they don't like someone, but it is awful to actually say the words. Four years have passed since this argument, and I have learned some very valuable lessons. You can't make people happy, they have to do it for themselves. You can't make people love you or even an innocent child. And giving birth does not make you a mother…unconditional love does.

I have pledged to myself that when my children marry, I won't meddle in their lives. My mother's mother-in-law meddled in her life so she made the same pledge to herself, and she never interferes with my marriage. My mother is the best grandma, mother, and mother-in-law a person could have. When I moved away from home, my mother told me to love my mother-in-law like I loved her. She told me to go to her for advice and to develop a strong bond with her. And when I did that, I was stabbed in the back. That is the only bad advice my mother has ever given me. The rest is solid gold. And if you have a good mother-in-law, then it's not bad advice at all!

LISTEN UP MOTHERS-IN-LAW

My mother-in-law…Much to be said, but I think I will start with a small story that took place at the beginning of our marriage.

1. I forgot to mention the groom's parents in our Wedding Announcement. (Big Mistake)
2. They ate Ukrainian food, and I was always afraid to invite them over for dinner. Then one day, she told me that she was coming over for dinner when I was planning on serving hot-dogs. After pouring over cookbooks and cleaning our very moldy house, I decided to cook Cornish Game Hens. Turns out, they both hate Cornish Game Hens and during dinner drinks she said, "You don't like cleaning much?" This house was so bad that we had to pick off the mushrooms growing along the tub and sink. No amount of cleaning could make this shack presentable.

That all happened during the first few years of our marriage. Now, fifteen years later, she still thinks she runs the show. I have finally showed some backbone, but this can result in losing the relationships I have developed with most of my husband's side of the family. I used to have great respect for her over the years, but I only realized recently that she still does not think I am worthy of her family. This can cost her the son she relies on greatly (who has also seen this "new" side of her) and time. The time she has with her grandchildren. Which should be precious to her. I only wish that she could see us as the good people we are, and enjoy her grandkids. Both of my children are married, and I hope that I am not interfering in their marriages unless of course, they ask me to. A message to all mothers-in-law: You will lose more than you will gain by not letting your child's spouse be your friend and respecting them for the care they provide to your son, grandchildren, and maybe to you one day. Let go and try to enjoy them. Then they will always be there when you need them.

Part 10: Infamous Lines

I do not think this section needs a long introduction. Infamous Lines are usually nothing more than a rude comment or action that your mother-in-law does to you when she feels like it. For instance, you may be sitting at dinner with her, and she asks you to pass the rolls. "Can you pass the rolls to me, you sure don't need to have another one." As you are passing the basket to her, it suddenly hits you that she just insulted you. You see, these are the comments and actions that are rude enough to anger you, but too insignificant to make a big deal out of.

- My mother-in-law is unbelievable. As a wedding gift, she gave us a book on how not to have failed marriage.
- My ex-mother-in-law use to make me pay her $6.00 an hour to watch her grandchild.
- My former mother-in-law named a giant sow after me, and it wasn't even her prize sow!
- My mother-in-law suggested that I should stand on a chair for my wedding pictures. I was simply too short!
- My mother-in-law calls everyday to make sure the kids are still alive!
- My mother-in-law told my husband that if he married me, he was no longer her son. How exactly does that happen?
- My mother-in-law told me that I should put my dogs to sleep because they are too much of a financial burden on us.
- After I had a miscarriage, my mother-in-law exclaimed, "You didn't need that baby anyway!"

- My mother-in-law took my daughter shopping for her tenth birthday. When they came home, my mother-in-law told me how unfortunate it was that my daughter inherited my pear-shaped body.

- My mother-in-law told me that when she first met me, she was a little worried that her son was gay. The reason; she thought I was a man because of my short hair and stocky build.

- My mother-in-law asked me to lie and tell her friends that I was Jewish. She couldn't possibly tell them that her son married a Catholic girl.

- When I told my mother-in-law that my mother was from Argentina, she said that she would not like her because women from that country are rude and have no class. Personally, I think it's the other way around!

- When I told my mother-in-law that my parents were divorced, she said, "You know, your marriage has very little chance of lasting. The rate of divorce is much higher when one spouse comes from a broken home."

Daughter-in-law Creed

When I was writing this book, one woman asked me, "I was wondering if your relationship with your mother-in-law has gotten any better. If so, how? What was your magic?" At first, I was a little taken back by the question, and I will admit that I got a bit defensive. If I told her that I have not spoken to my mother-in-law for over a year, would she think that I was a flake for writing this book? Wasn't I supposed to try and help women make amends with their mother-in-law? Every book I read tried to give me tips on how to be a good daughter-in-law or how to get along with her. For instance, one book I read said that if your mother-in-law says something that you disagree with, it is best not to say anything. This would just cause unnecessary conflict between the two of you.

Their advice is that we should hold in our feelings, so we don't upset our mother-in-law? That is all fine and dandy if you want to have her walk all over you for the rest of your life! I needed advice on how to have a happy marriage when your mother-in-law can't stand you and probably never will. I could not find this kind of book anywhere. With the millions of books that fill the shelves of bookstores, why hasn't anyone written about this very prevalent problem? Well I believe that this daughter-in-law/mother-in-law struggle is a dirty little secret that no one wants to bring up. Instead, daughters-in-law are forced to suffer in silence and let their mothers-in-law have all the power. I don't agree with this philosophy. Maybe this is why my mother-in-law doesn't like me.

So for my fellow daughter-in-law who asked me if I have a better relationship with my mother-in-law, here is your answer: In all honesty, my relationship with my mother-in-law is nonexistent as of right now. I did everything in my power to find a middle ground with her, but her only middle ground was to have her son move back home and divorce me! That was something both my husband and I were not willing to do. I tried everything to get along with her. Sometimes, I even sacrificed my beliefs so I could stay in her good graces. After several years of biting my tongue, I realized that she still did not like me. For some reason, she made up her mind that I was not good enough for her son, and there was nothing I could ever do to change that. I can almost accept that now. Sometimes, no advice in the world will make your mother-in-law change the way she feels about you. This is why we should try to find comfort and peace of mind knowing that we are not alone in this.

TIPS TO GETTING ALONG WITH YOUR MOTH-ER-IN-LAW

Since I don't want to come off like a mother-in-law basher, I thought I should include some tips on "How To Get Along With Your Mother-In-Law." Maybe you see your mother-in-law as a diamond in the rough. If you have not made any attempts to salvage your relationship with her, then you are hurting yourself and your husband. Take it from me, I would much rather be on good terms with her. It would make my life so much easier. I would not have to feel guilty for getting between my husband and his mother. Nor would I have to get a knot in my stomach from the mere mention of her name. However, I have already tried to make amends, and it did not work. At least I made the effort. So go ahead and try out these tips. What do you have to lose?

Never forget her Birthday

The worst thing that you can do is to forget her birthday. This shows her how important she is in your life. Would you forget your own mother's birthday?

Invite her to your home

You mother-in-law should not have to invite herself over to your home. By extending an invitation to her, she will feel that you are making time for her in your life.

Try not to take vacations on her son's Birthday or Holidays

Your mother-in-law has probably celebrated every birthday and holiday with her son. If you come along and take him away on these special days, this may cause her to resent you.

Make an effort to include your mother-in-law in important family matters

When you married her son, she probably felt like she was losing him to you. A mother will always want to play an important role in her child's life. By including her in your family matters, she will not feel like an outsider.

Do not make a big deal over the small things she might say or do to you

Try not to go head to head with her whenever she says or does something that bothers you. If you plan on staying married to your husband for the rest of your life, do you really feel like fighting with this woman all the time? If you let the small stuff slide by and only react when she says or does something that truly disturbs you, she will know that you mean business.

HOW TO HANDLE A TROUBLESOME MOTHER-IN-LAW

She is always telling you how to live your life

The best thing you can do is to be honest with her. Tell her that you really do appreciate her advice, and you will think about what she has said. Then let her know your views on the subject. Be honest but not harsh.

She can't admit when she is wrong

Some people think they are always right, even if the truth is staring them in the face. No one likes to admit their mistakes, and it can definitely be frustrating for the other party. If your mother-in-law refuses to acknowledge that she did something wrong to you, then it is up to you to forgive her. You can try to fight with her, but where is that going to get you? You will both feel angry and nothing will be resolved. It can be hard to forgive someone who did not offer an apology, but you will need to. You will be the bigger person and feel better about yourself.

She is always interfering in your marriage

This can be a tricky one to handle. First, it is very hard to step back from a situation and not become involved. We are all guilty of this. Maybe we do not want our loved ones to repeat the same mistakes we did, so we voice our opinions. Sometimes, we become militant. This could very well be the same case for your mother-in-law. What you may perceive as being nosy and bossy is perhaps her way of trying to guide you and your husband in the right path. However, if you feel that she is becoming too involved in your marriage, I would suggest having your husband talk to her about it. It is not your place to confront her. She will only become defensive and bitter towards you.

Note: These are just a few tips that I can remember trying out. If you think these could be the answer to your mother-in-law problems, then I suggest buying a book that focuses on ways to improve your relationship with her. Now if you rolled your eyes even one time to these suggestions, I bet you have already tried these tips plus many more, and they did not work. Hey, join the club! And if this is the case, then you can always rip out this page and go back to the Daughter-in-law Creed.

A MOTHER-IN-LAW GETS THE LAST WORD

You may be very proud of the book you have written. You may have had the mother-in-law from hell, if so, I feel very sorry for you. I had the mother-in-law from heaven and the daughter-in-law from hell. Many studies on relationships between mothers-in-law and daughters-in-law have proven that in many instances, the daughter-in-law is usually the one at fault. She usually begins by cutting off the son from his mother by using deceitful methods. When that happened to me, I just let it happen because I knew that my son would take his wife's side. After less than a year, he came to tell me that he finally realized that the problem between his wife and me was not of my making but hers. That was a happy day for me. They remained married for about fifteen years after that, but now they are divorced. I stayed away from her. Fortunately for me, my son brought his two children to see me often, and we all have a great relationship. The ex-daughter-in-law called me after the divorce and told me that she never liked me because I could see right through her. Which was true. She was always less than honest.

Signed,
A battered mother-in-law.

PS. Perhaps, you will do some more research and write a book about the pain that many mothers-in-law must endure because of selfish daughters-in-law. I received that story just days after I wrote my final thoughts. I contemplated leaving it out, but then I thought it would be fair to let a mother-in-law speak her mind. Now I leave it up to you to decide whether or not she is truly a battered mother-in-law or just another mother-in-law from hell!

EPILOGUE

Before you close this book, I want to make sure that everyone understands why I wrote it in the first place. I did not think that I would become the next Pulitzer Prize winner, nor do I expect to make a fortune from it. However, I am hoping that this book will help daughters-in-law realize that many other women are struggling with the same feelings of anger, guilt, blame, and sadness. Also, I am optimistic that some mothers-in-law will read this book too, and recognize similar behavior patterns that they share with the women that these stories are based upon. I never believed this notion was possible until I received the following letter from a mother who did not want to be the next mother-in-law from hell.

"I have had the same mother-in-law for thirty years, and she has never once acknowledged that her grandchildren or I have birthdays'. Apparently, only she and her son have them!! She telephones every night at the same time (thank God for caller ID). If no one is home, she leaves a message always addressed to just her son and not to the rest of the family who may be listening to the message. Unfortunately, my son is marrying a girl that I am not particularly fond of and probably never will be. I certainly do not want to become one of those "Mothers-In-Law from Hell!" I wish it were easier to pretend to like someone that you really do not have a single good feeling about! Maybe reading your book about some of awful things that mothers-in-law have done, I can prevent myself from ending up in your next book!" The woman who submitted that story knew how it felt to be disliked by a mother-in-law, and she is making a conscious effort to not start off on the wrong foot with her future daughter-in-law. Even though she is not too fond of the woman her son has chosen to marry, she is well aware of the consequences that all parties involved may face if she shows her discontent.

I know it may sound like I am warning mothers-in-law to like their daughters-in-law or they will lose everything. Trust me, I am not by any means insinuating that daughters-in-law are perfect. Although I would like to think that we can do no wrong, I believe we all know that this is simply untrue. Honestly, if I could do everything over again, maybe I would have changed some of the things I said to her, and the actions I took. I am sure that I was overly defensive at times and maybe a fight that ignited was my fault once or twice! I am just kidding. It was more like three or four times.

Seriously, we are human, and we are bound to make mistakes. But we do not need to have them thrown in our face for the rest of our lives. We do not deserve to be talked down to, ridiculed, embarrassed, or made to feel guilty by our mothers-in-law. And the daughter-in-law needs to remember that your mother-in-law is not made of stone, it is essential for you to consider her feelings too. Remember, she thinks that she has done nothing wrong. Now, imagine how frustrating it must be for her.

In closing, I can only wish that when we become mothers-in-law, we will have a little more compassion for the women our sons' marry. We will know first hand how it feels to have a meddling mother-in-law, and we should not want to inflict that torture on any living creature. Some of us will have the good fortune of having a daughter-in-law whom we would have handpicked ourselves. Then, there will be some mothers who cringe at the very sight of their daughter-in-law. It is inevitable, and that is the way life goes. However, we should have a better understanding on how to handle the relationship and learn to role with the punches.

If we are aware of the circumstances and can keep the peace, then our children will learn from us. Then they can pass it on to the next generation and so on. Who knows…maybe in the next few centuries, the mother-in-law/daughter-in-law feud will be a subject that women can only read about. Wouldn't that be a nice thought?